NICA GUIDE TO THE SOCIAL SCIENCES

ORIOGRAPHY

EDITED BY
ZOE LOWERY

Britannica®
Educational Pu

IN ASSOCIATION

ROSE
EDUCATIONAL SE

D1364629

Published in 2016 by Britannica Educational Publishing (a trademark of Encyclopædia Britannica, Inc.) in association with The Rosen Publishing Group, Inc.
29 East 21st Street, New York, NY 10010

Britannica Educational Publishing
J.E. Luebering: Director, Core Reference Group
Anthony L. Green: Editor, Compton's by Britannica

Rosen Publishing
Zoe Lowery: Editor
Nelson Sá: Art Director
Brian Garvey: Designer
Cindy Reiman: Photography Manager
Karen Huang: Photo Researcher
Portions of the introduction and supplementary material by Marcia Amidon Lusted.

Cataloging-in-Publication Data
Historiography / edited by Zoe Lowery.
     pages cm. — (Britannica guide to social sciences)
Includes bibliographical references and index.
ISBN 978-1-62275-560-8 (library bound : alk. paper)
1. Historiography. 2. Historiography—History. I. Lowery, Zoe, editor.

D13.H566 2015
907.2—dc23

2015021750

Manufactured in the United States of America.

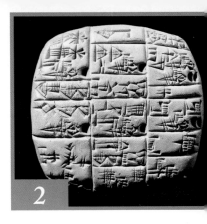

2

11

23

127

130

149

INTRODUCTION

I n some ways, it can be said that historiography is the *history* of history. It is not so much about what happened, but more about how a historical event has been written about, and how that changes depending on who is doing the writing. In most cases it refers to the writing of history, especially the writing of history based on looking critically at sources, how particular details have been selected from the authentic materials in those sources, and how those details are synthesized into a narrative that can stand up to critical examination. Basically, it focuses on writing about history and not just looking at the details of chronologies and events. It is the literature, methodologies, and guidelines for the best practices in writing about history. The term *historiography* also refers to the theory and history of historical writing.

Modern historians try to reconstruct a record of human activities and then achieve a more profound understanding of them. This concept of what historians do is actually quite recent, dating from the development in the late 18th and early 19th centuries of "scientific" history and, at the same time, the rise of history as an academic profession. Even though people have always thought about history, especially in terms of their own experience, history itself was never considered to be a formal area of study. Making it into one springs from an outlook that is very new in human experience: realizing that the study of history really is a natural, inevitable human activity. Before the late 18th century, historiography did not play an important role in Western civilization. History was almost never a part of regular education, and it never claimed to provide a way to interpret human life as a whole. People were more apt to consider the meaning of human life as something that was more appropriate to religion, philosophy, and perhaps poetry and other imaginative literature.

All human cultures tell stories about the past. Deeds of ancestors, heroes, gods, or animals sacred to a particular people were chanted and memorized long before there was any way to record them in writing. By

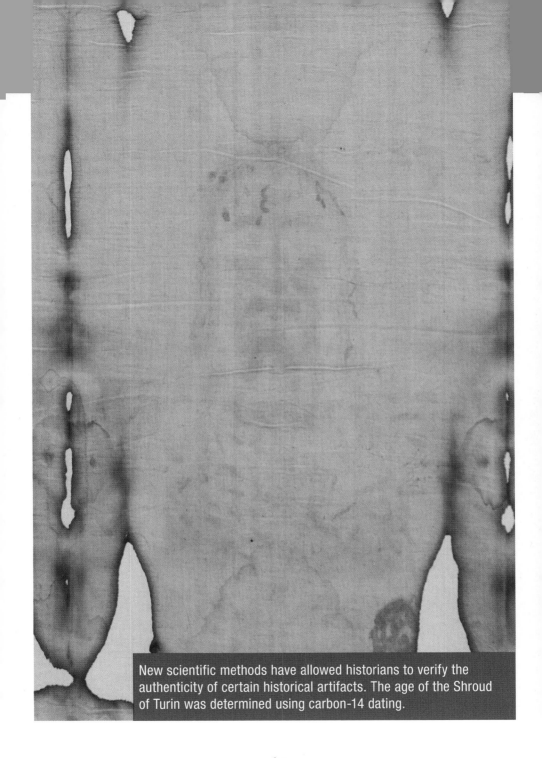

New scientific methods have allowed historians to verify the authenticity of certain historical artifacts. The age of the Shroud of Turin was determined using carbon-14 dating.

repeating these stories of the past over and over again, they became a true and authentic part of the culture even without being written down. History, which may be defined as a story or narrative that claims to be a true account of events and ways of thinking and feeling in some part of the human past, comes from this original, natural human storytelling activity.

With its origins as storytelling in cultures that did not have a written language, history shares a common ancestry with myth, legend, epic poetry, and the novel. But history has of course diverged from these forms of literature. Its claim to truth is based in part on the fact that all the persons or events it describes really existed or occurred at some time in the past. Anything that historians say about these persons or events must be able to be supported by research based on some kind of documentary evidence. This evidence usually takes the form of something written, such as a letter, a law, an administrative record, or the account written by some previous historian. Historians may also, at times, create their own evidence by interviewing people and using their oral histories and accounts of their own experiences. In the 20th century, the scope of historical evidence became even wider and began to include, among many other things, such unusual evidence as aerial photographs, the rings of trees, old coins, clothes, motion pictures, and houses. There are also new scientific methods to aid historians in authenticating historical artifacts. For example, modern historians have determined the actual age of the Shroud of Turin, which supposedly bears the image of Jesus, through carbon-14 dating. They have also discredited Anna Anderson's claim that she is the grand duchess Anastasia, the daughter of Tsar Nicholas II, by the use of DNA testing.

Just as the methods at the disposal of historians have expanded, so have the subjects in which they have become interested. Many of the indigenous peoples of Africa, the Americas, and Polynesia, for example, were long dismissed by Europeans as having no precolonial history because they did not keep written records before the arrival of European explorers. In fact, it was sometimes said that Africa south of the Sahara desert had no civilization and so no history. There was also the argument that even if these places did have historical events, the fact that there were no written sources or narratives made this history unknowable and so impossible to verify and study. The only knowledge of these areas came from classical sources, which were not focused or organized, and then from Islamic and Arabic writers. Later, as these areas were colonized, European writers, travelers, and missionaries wrote about them from their own perspectives. Such writing often reflected the attitude that places like Africa were savage and untamed and needed the beneficent influence of Europe and other "civilized" countries. The idea that history did not exist without written sources was a very European-centric perspective, and it was not until these areas ceased to be colonies of European powers and gained independence that this perspective began to shift. However, sophisticated study of oral traditions, using the same rigorous and disciplined use of sources and multidisciplinary methods drawn from archaeology, ethnography, anthropology, linguistics, and art history, has made it possible to discover a good deal about the civilizations and empires that flourished in these regions before European contact.

Historians have also studied new social classes. The earliest histories were mostly stories of disasters—floods, famines, and plagues—or of wars, including the statesmen and generals who played important roles during them. In the 20th century, however, historians shifted their focus from statesmen and generals to ordinary workers and soldiers. Until relatively recent times, however, most men and virtually all women were excluded from history because they were unable to write. Virtually all that was known about them passed through the often inaccurate filter of the attitudes of the literate elite class of people. The challenge of seeing through that filter has been met by historians in various ways. One way is to make use of nontraditional sources—for example, personal documents, such as journals, letters, wills, or marriage contracts. Another is to look at the records of individual towns and cities rather than of central governments.

Through these means even the most oppressed peoples—African American slaves or medieval heretics, for example—have had at least some of their history restored. Since the 20th century some historians have also become interested in psychological repression—in attitudes and actions that might require psychological insight and even diagnosis to recover and understand. For the first time, the claim of historians to deal with the feelings as well as the thoughts of people in any part of the human past has been made good.

None of this is to say that history writing has reached a perfect or completed form. It never will: examination of its past reveals remarkable changes in how people think about history, rather than uninterrupted progress toward the standards of research and writing that represent the best that historians can do today. Changes in thinking about history generally have not been steady and gradual. Instead, they have been relatively abrupt, created by events such as the quest for racial and gender equality and by the realization that history is also ordinary people, not just those who win the battles and create the policies.

Writing about history is also influenced by the person who is doing the writing. Several historians can view the same set of facts and reach different conclusions. For example, someone who is writing about the events of the Vietnam War and was alive during the conflict is apt to have a much different perspective from someone who is writing about it without ever having been directly affected by the actual events. It is also a well-known fact, and one that is taken into account in courts of law, that two eyewitnesses to an event will often have two entirely different accounts of what took place, and the same is true of historical interpretation. Also, most historians are thinking about a specific problem or historical question when they write. They are also writing through their own specific worldview or perspective. This is part of human nature; we see the world through our own experiences and the knowledge we have of other people's experiences.

Specific questions must be addressed when evaluating a work of history. First of all, who is writing it, and with what purpose in mind? How is the perspective of that historian colored by factors such as gender, age, nationality, or ideology? What types of primary and secondary sources has the historian chosen to use? Do those sources prejudice the outcome of the historian's work?

When evaluating historical writing about a particular topic, it is necessary to consider several points. The essential arguments and interpretations of the sources are considered, as well as how scholars have framed their questions about the topic and what assumptions and perspectives might be influencing their approach. It is also important to identify the methodologies used to examine the sources. Evaluators must determine whether there are other sources, perspectives, or viewpoints missing from the written work they are examining, and whether that factor affects the strength of the arguments being made.

Modern historiography seeks to minimize bias and prejudice while organizing sources and information into patterns and creating new interpretations and narratives. Accordingly, it is fair to say that 21st-century historians understand the pasts of more people more completely and more accurately than did their predecessors. Indeed, it is fascinating to see just how far historiography has come and to trace the process through which that understanding has been achieved. Historiography has moved from narratives created by rulers and victors or focusing on those deemed most important to a more balanced perspective that includes a wider range of people and viewpoints.

CHAPTER ONE

IN THE BEGINNING

I n the beginning was the spoken word. Humans lived for tens of thousands of years with language, and thus with tales about the past, but without writing. Oral history is still important in all parts of the world, and successful transmission of stories over many generations suggests that people without writing can have a sophisticated historical sense. The historical record, however, must start with a system of writing and a suitable writing technology. The earliest forms of writing included cuneiform and pictographs, which were inscribed on stone and clay tablets in Egypt and Mesopotamia, as well as Chinese ideograms, which were incised in bronze and on oracle bones (baked oxen bones whose cracks and fissures were thought to foretell the future). People in Egypt, Mesopotamia, and China were the first to make records of their contemporaries, which took the form of lists of kings and ancestors.

EGYPT AND MESOPOTAMIA

In Egypt, the first lists date from about the middle of the 3rd millennium BCE and extend back another 1,000 years to a time when kings were thought to mingle with gods. Entries were made year by year, making these lists among the earliest annals. In addition to the names of kings, events occasionally are mentioned, especially for the later years; but it is hard to understand on what principle they are included. Sandwiched between notations of offerings to the gods are such enigmatic references as "Smiting of the cave dwellers." Despite their occasional obscurity,

Cuneiform tablet featuring a tally of sheep and goats, from Tello in Mesopotamia (present-day Iraq)

these early historians accomplished the considerable task of organizing the past into units of the same size (years) and assigning events to them.

The king-lists of the Sumerians, the oldest civilization in Mesopotamia, not only presented the order of rulers but described shifts in power as various kings were "smitten with weapons" and overthrown. The Sumerians were also capable of weaving events into a narrative. A Sumerian stela, or standing stone slab, dating from about 2,400 BCE records what is probably the world's first historical narrative. The Stele of the Vultures was erected by the city of Lagash to commemorate its victory in a boundary war with Umma; it contains depictions of warriors in battle gear and an inscription celebrating the triumph.

Sumerian writers seem to have developed their own interpretation of history. This interpretation is reflected in the preoccupation of the king-lists with the transitory nature of royal power and in the Sumerian belief that natural phenomena (notably the behaviour of the Euphrates River) are determined by the gods. Although Sumerian gods could be bungling and cowardly and sometimes even subject to fate, they retained the power to punish humans who offended them. The vicissitudes of kings and states were thought to demonstrate the gods' power to influence human affairs.

CHINA

A rich and persistent annalistic tradition and a growing emphasis on history as a repertoire of moral examples characterized the earliest Chinese historiography. The first Chinese historians were apparently temple archivists; as the bureaucratic structure of the Chinese state developed, historians occupied high offices. History gained prestige through the thought of the philosopher Confucius (551–479 BCE), who was traditionally—though probably wrongly—credited with writing the *Chunqiu* ("Spring and Autumn [Annals]") and the *Shujing* ("Classic of History"). As articulated in these works, Chinese historical thought was intensely moralistic: virtue was conceived as following the example of one's ancestors. There was consistent interest in the form of governing institutions and frequent emphasis on the doctrine of the Mandate of Heaven—the idea that a monarch ruled by heaven's decree, which would be withdrawn if he committed evil.

The foundational text of Chinese historiography is the *Shiji* ("Historical Records"), which was compiled by Sima Qian (c. 145–c. 86 BCE). It is an account of the entire history of China from mythical times through the establishment of the Han dynasty in 206 BCE. The story becomes more detailed as Sima Qian approaches his own time and is able to question eyewitnesses of events and make use of abundant official documents. Sima Qian introduced order into the welter of surviving records by organizing them into categories.

The classical Chinese historians made an ideal of objectivity. Although they eschewed interpretation of the historical record, they were often faced with conflicting sources. In such cases they typically chose only one, though they never referred to their sources or explained the choices they made. Historical criticism in China was constrained by propriety because of the high cultural value of ancestors; anything like the contentiousness of the Greeks would have been regarded as most unseemly.

By about 710 CE, however, Liu Zhiji (661–721) had produced the *Shitong* ("Historical Perspectives"), the first comprehensive work on historical criticism in any language. For him, the writing of history had an exalted—and very Confucian—mission:

> **Man lives in his bodily shape between heaven and earth and his life is like the span of the summer fly, like the passing of a white colt glimpsed through a crack in the wall. Yet he is shamed to think that within those years his merit will not be known…there is truly none who is not tireless in pursuing merit and fame.…Why is this? Because all have their heart set on immortality. And what, then, is immortality? No more than to have one's name written in a book.**

Liu Zhiji's view had a lasting influence. Indeed, some of his maxims are still recommended to beginning historians: skepticism about the sources, freedom from deference to established scholars, the necessity of extensive knowledge of the sources before selection can be made, and insistence on arguments supported by extensive evidence.

HEBREW TRADITIONS

The Hebrew Bible (Old Testament) was as fundamental to Western historiography as the dynastic histories were to Chinese historiography. Although the Bible is many things, it is substantially a work of history. Seventeen of its 39 books are historical, and the 5 major and 12 minor prophets also offer moral interpretations of historical events. Furthermore, references in the Hebrew Bible indicate that annals of the Israelite kings once existed, though they have since been lost.

A creation story, an account of a flood that all but destroys humanity, long genealogical lists, a set of laws or commandments, and reflections on the effects of divine wrath on the prosperity of kings and peoples can be found among other Western Asian peoples. Nevertheless, the so-called Yahwist writer (one of the individuals or groups identified as a source of the Torah or Pentateuch, the first five books of the Hebrew Bible) possessed a unique conception of history, and the Hebrews identified themselves as a distinct people only because of that conception. They alone had entered into a covenant with Yahweh, who promised Abraham, the first of the Hebrew patriarchs, that his descendants would be as numerous as the sands of the sea. The Hebrews believed that the hand of Yahweh had led them to escape bondage in Egypt and eventually to subdue the peoples of Palestine in order to occupy the Promised Land.

That land was ill-chosen as a peaceful place to live. The Hebrews faced the constant threat of being squeezed between the great powers of the region. About 722 BCE the northern kingdom of Israel fell to the Assyrians, and about 598 BCE the southern kingdom of Judah was conquered by the Babylonians, who carried many Hebrews off to captivity; the Babylonian Exile lasted until 538 BCE, when the Persian conquerors of Babylonia allowed the Hebrews to return to Jerusalem. The authors of the Hebrew Bible did not, however, think in geopolitical terms; they tried instead to understand why the promise, which seemed to guarantee earthly success, had apparently been abrogated by Yahweh.

Agonizing over this problem led to something hitherto unknown: a widespread reconception of the historical record. The compilers of the Hebrew scriptures had already rejected the sort of vainglorious boasting characteristic of the records of Babylonian kings. The succession story of King David, for example, does not spare details of his discreditable actions. More serious than any individual sin, however, were the sins committed by the Hebrew people as a whole, who are depicted on occasion as turning away from the worship of Yahweh. It was not unusual

5

to see in the disasters that overwhelmed them the avenging hand of Yahweh, but what required historical reflection was the task of reconciling the apostasy and its punishment with the continuing validity of the promise made to Abraham. Eventually the major prophets, especially Isaiah, reinterpreted the story of their people. Despite the sins and sufferings of the people of Yahweh, the promise had not been invalidated and could even be renewed, because the people's destiny had not been world power or even a secure kingdom. Instead they had been chosen to suffer as a servant of all of humanity.

This view was distinctive in being a history not merely of a single king or dynasty but of a people. Furthermore, it was not narrowly nationalistic; it extended back to the beginnings of the human race and showed how Yahweh, the Lord of the whole earth, was working out his divine plan for humanity through his promise to the chosen people. Unlike the historical vision of other Western Asian peoples, which had seldom extended far into the past or beyond their own ethnic group, the view of the Hebrews was in principle universal. Because the promise was capable of redefinition and renewal, there was even a rudimentary notion of history as progressive.

One element of modern historical scholarship that does not appear in the works of Western Asian peoples is criticism of sources. Babylonian records often end with elaborate curses against anyone who would seek to alter them. It was the classical Greek historians who first made a systematic attempt to find out what actually happened, rather than to preserve a traditional record of events.

GREEK HISTORIOGRAPHY

Greek historiography originated in the activities of a group of writers whom the Greeks called *logographoi* ("logographers"). Logography was the prose compilation of oral traditions relating to the origins of towns, peoples, and places. It combined geographical with cultural information and might be seen as an early form of cultural anthropology. Hecataeus of Miletus, the best known of the logographers, defined his task in his *Genealogia* (c. 490 BCE) as follows: "I write what I consider the truth, for the things the Greeks tell us are in my opinion full of contradictions and worthy to be laughed out of court." The logographers also served as advocates and speech writers in the courts, and the need to ascertain facts and make arguments clearly influenced their writings.

HERODOTUS

Although the logographers pioneered in the study of history, their influence was eclipsed by Herodotus, who has been called the "father of history." His "History" of the Greco-Persian Wars is the longest extant text in ancient Greek. The fact that it has survived when so many other works written in ancient Greece were lost, including the majority of the plays of the great tragedians (Aeschylus, Euripides, and Sophocles) and much of the corpus of Aristotle), is testimony to the great esteem in which it was held.

Like the logographers, Herodotus's approach was historical and anthropological. He questioned the priests at Memphis (in Egypt) and those at Heliopolis and Thebes "expressly to try whether the priests of those places [Heliopolis and Thebes] would agree in their accounts with the priests at Memphis." He discovered that the Egyptian historical records went much further back than the Greek ones and that Egyptian customs were the reverse of those he knew (which he called "the common practice of mankind"). The Egyptians ate no wheat or barley; kneaded dough with their feet but mixed mud or even dung with their hands; lived with animals; and wrote from right to left. Herodotus also observed that "women attend the markets and trade, while the men sit at home at the loom."

Although Herodotus also gave ethnographic details of this kind on the Scythians and the Persians, his "History" possesses a narrative thread, which he announces in the first paragraph: "These are the

THUCYDIDES

As long as the subject of history is studied, the fame of the Athenian Thucydides (460?–404? BCE) will be secure. His stature as a historian has never been surpassed and is rarely equaled. His *History of the Peloponnesian War* was the first recorded political and moral analysis of a nation's war policies.

Of his life very little is known beyond what he reports in the book itself. He was in Athens during a serious outbreak of plague in 430 and 429 BCE, and in 424 he was elected a military magistrate and given command of a fleet. Because he failed to prevent the capture of the city of Amphipolis by the Spartans, he was recalled, tried, and sentenced to exile. Thus he was away from Athens for most of the rest of the war (the war lasted from 431 to 404). For the purposes of his history, this exile gave him the chance for travel and wider contacts among the various combatants, especially in Sparta. His exile ended with the defeat of Athens by Sparta in 404. It is presumed that he died about that time

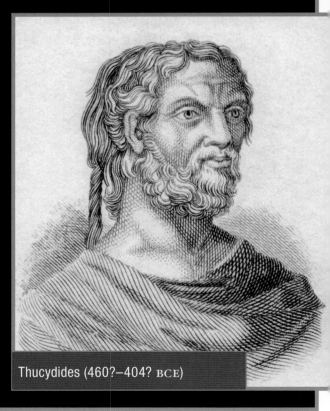

Thucydides (460?–404? BCE)

because his history is incomplete; it ends in 411.

From the *History* it is assumed that Thucydides worked in three stages: making notes of events as they occurred, reworking them into a narrative, and finally elaborating the narrative into the full history. The "History" treats all aspects of the war, including its technical problems, logistics, sieges, and other military features. It is also about individual personalities, the political and military leadership, and, significantly, the behavior of peoples as the long war dragged on.

researches of Herodotus of Halicarnassus, which he publishes, in the hope of thereby preserving from decay the remembrance of what men have done, and of preventing the great and wonderful actions of the Greeks and the barbarians from losing their due meed of glory; and withal to put on record what were their grounds of feud." The "grounds of feud" are traced back beyond the Trojan War (12th or 13th century BCE) to a series of abductions of women by both Europeans and Asians. The Greeks made themselves enemies of Persia (which claimed all of Asia) when they led an army to besiege the Anatolian city of Troy to recover Helen, the Greek woman kidnapped by the Trojan prince Paris. The rivalry was renewed in the time of the Persian king Xerxes, leading to an epic conflict between the enormous forces of Persia and those of Athens, Sparta, and most, though not all, of the other Greek city-states. The pattern of a nemesis upon the hubris of the Persians is obvious.

Despite his apparently conscientious questioning of his witnesses, Herodotus developed a reputation for credulity. However, although he was certainly not one to resist a good story, he did not endorse everything he reported. He described a story that the Greeks told about the mythical hero Heracles as a "silly fable" that reflected badly on their critical sense. In the tradition of the logographers, he believed that his duty was to record the traditions of various peoples, no matter how dubious. He combined a remarkable narrative artistry with an effort to discern the causes of customs and events.

ROMAN HISTORIOGRAPHY

The Romans inherited Greek historiography as they inherited other elements of Greek culture, aware of its prestige and emulating it in some ways but inevitably giving it the imprint of their quite different temperament. Fittingly, it was a Greek writing in Greek, Polybius (c. 200–c. 118 BCE), who first offered key insights into the development of the Roman state and discussed aspects of Roman society that the Romans themselves had hardly noticed.

POLYBIUS

Polybius asked: "Can anyone be so indifferent or idle as not to care to know by what means, and under what kind of polity, almost the whole inhabited world was conquered and brought under the domination of the single city of Rome, and that too within a period of not quite 53 years?" In answering this question, Polybius drew comparisons between the Romans and the Greeks, the latter of whom failed to forge a lasting empire, even under Alexander the Great (356–323 BCE). The primary reason for Rome's success, according to Polybius, was the Roman character, as reflected in statesmanship, public spirit, and moderation toward defeated peoples.

Polybius also argued that Roman political institutions were superior to Greek ones. He accepted the theory of the cyclical degeneration and regeneration of Greek city-states, which had been elaborated by Aristotle. This theory maintained that city-states develop first as despotisms and

Polybius, statue in Vienna

evolve through periods of monarchy, tyranny, aristocracy, oligarchy, democracy and finally mob rule before the restoration of order in a new despotism. There was, however, nothing inevitable about this cycle, and Polybius at one time believed that the Romans might avert it because the constitution of the Roman Republic was mixed, allowing for some monarchical and some popular elements as well as the aristocracy of the Senate. (This theory of the benefits of mixed government was to have a long career.) Finally, Polybius believed the Romans had been favored by *Tyche* ("fate" or "fortune"), which was partly responsible for drawing the world under Roman rule.

Like Thucydides, Polybius relied on personal experience and the cross-examination of eyewitnesses. Thus, he retraced the route of the Carthaginian general Hannibal across the Alps and observed the siege of Carthage in 146 BCE. Although he scorned historians who merely sat in their studies, he also condemned petty histories of small corners of the world. To the contrary, the triumph of Rome called for a universal history: "Up to this time the world's history had been, so to speak, a series of disconnected transactions....But from this time forth History becomes a connected whole: the affairs of Italy and Libya are involved with those of Asia and Greece, and the tendency of all is to unity."

DIODORUS, SALLUST, AND LIVY

Unfortunately, a method based on personal experience and eyewitness accounts could capture a moment of decisive conquest but could not yield universal history. It remained for Diodorus Siculus in the 1st century BCE to come closest, among ancient writers, to this ideal. Diodorus traced to 60 BCE the histories of Arabs, Assyrians, Egyptians, Ethiopians, Greeks, Indians, Romans, and Scythians—not to mention Amazons and the residents of Atlantis. He is one of the main ancient supporters of the claim that Plato and other Greek thinkers learned their wisdom from the Egyptians.

Less than a century after Polybius explained the rise of the Roman state, Roman historians were beginning to speak of its decline. Sallust (c. 86–c. 35/34 BCE) described the conspiracy of the Roman patrician Catiline in the *Bellum Catilinae* (43–42 BCE; *Catiline's War*), and his *Bellum Jugurthinum* (41–40 BCE; *The Jugurthine War*) focused on the war against Jugurtha, the king of Numida (roughly present-day Algeria). The lesson of both was that the republic was rotting inwardly through corruption and the arrogance of power. Indeed, in Sallust's systematic analysis Rome was shown to be suffering the general fate of empires.

Livy (59/64 BCE–17 CE), one of the greatest Roman historians, lived through the fall of the republic and the establishment of the principate by Augustus, the first Roman emperor. Like Sallust, Livy was inclined to idealize the severe virtues of republican Rome. His monumental history, most of which has not survived, starts with the founding of the city and extends into the rule of Augustus. Like the *Aeneid*, by the Roman poet Virgil, Livy's work served to memorialize Rome's early history just as the republic was being transformed into an empire.

TACITUS

Nobody was more aware of this development, or decline, than Tacitus (56–120). His two great works—the *Annals*, which covers the years 14–68 CE, and the *Histories*, which begins with the famous "year of the four emperors" (69 CE) and ends with the death of the emperor Domitian (96)—provide an important account of the first century of the principate. Tacitus was a self-conscious stylist, and in his treatise on style he claimed that styles were themselves the product of historical changes rather than being entirely the decision of the historian. His own writing is perhaps most remarkable for its concise epigrams. Of the short-lived reign of the emperor Galba, for example, Tacitus wrote: "Capax imperium, nisi imperasset" ("He would have been capable of ruling, except that he ruled"). And concerning Roman methods of pacification, he observed, "Solitudinem faciunt, pacem appelant" ("They have made a desert and call it peace").

Politics, as it had been known in the republic, no longer existed; the intrigues of the imperial family and of its bodyguard, the Praetorian Guard, determined the fate of Rome. Instead of creating a master narrative about the impersonal forces that might have led to this development, as Polybius or even Sallust might have done, Tacitus focused on the character of the various emperors. As was typical of ancient authors, he had no conception of character as developing through the course of a lifetime. Innate character, however, reveals itself fully only in crises, or when the possession of absolute power allows all its latent features to emerge—as with the vanity and cruelty of Nero. Tacitus's emphasis upon character, despite the crudity of his psychological theories, made him a pioneer of psychohistory. It also brought the form of historical works close to that of multiple biographies.

SUETONIUS AND PLUTARCH

This is even more true of the *De vita Caesarum (Lives of the Caesars)*, written by Suetonius in the 2nd century. His treatments consist of an account of each emperor's administrative and military accomplishments followed by a description of his character and personal life. Although Suetonius, a former imperial secretary, drew upon the imperial archives in composing his "Lives," the work is best known for the scandalous details it provides regarding the private lives of the emperors. In this he differed from the best-known of the ancient biographers, Plutarch, whose *Bioi paralloi (Parallel Lives)* juxtaposed the life stories of 24 Romans and 24 Greeks who had faced similar experiences. His purpose was to draw moral lessons from the lives of these figures. If they responded differently to their challenges, it was partly a consequence of character, but weaknesses of character could—and should—be overcome by a strenuous exercise of virtue.

CHAPTER TWO

MEDIEVAL AND RENAISSANCE HISTORIOGRAPHY

The earliest Christians thought that history was about to end because Jesus had said that some of his disciples would still be alive at his Second Coming. Fired with such apocalyptic expectations, all they needed to know of history was that God had broken into it through the Incarnation and that Jesus had conquered death through the Resurrection. Thus, it was hardly inevitable that Christians would develop an interest in history, much less their own philosophy of history. But the authors of the canonical Gospels (Matthew, Mark, Luke, and John) regarded the Hebrew Bible as authoritative and reinterpreted it to accord with the new revelation. In their view many prophecies of the Hebrew scriptures referred to Jesus, and many of its stories prefigured his life (thus, Jonah's three-day sojourn in the belly of the great fish was a foreshadowing of the Resurrection).

Incorporation of the Hebrew Bible into the Christian canon helped to shape the Christian conception of history. By tracing their history to Adam and Eve and the other figures who preceded Abraham, Christians encompassed all of humanity within their worldview. Reflecting the influence of the Hebrew prophets, the early Christians held that sins were inevitably followed by divine punishment and that the plot of history was the unfolding of God's will for humanity. Disasters represented punishment for sins; prosperity indicated divine favor to faithful humans. Thus, nothing could happen that could not be explained by the providential interpretation of history.

Nevertheless, the idea of providence did not instantly solve all historical problems, some of which were peculiar to Christianity. In particular, what was the place of the Roman Empire in the divine plan? For almost three centuries Christians provoked in Roman authorities puzzlement, exasperation, and intermittent persecution. For their part, Christians treated the empire as at best irrelevant and at worst (as in the Revelation to John) as one of the beasts of the apocalypse. But with the conversion of the emperor Constantine in 312, Christian historians had to come to terms with the historical significance of a Christian emperor. The challenge was met by Eusebius, whose *Historia ecclesiastica* (written 312–324; *Ecclesiastical History*) was the first important work of Christian history since the Acts of the Apostles. For Eusebius, the Roman Empire was the divinely appointed and necessary milieu for the propagation of the Christian faith. Roman peace and Roman roads allowed the Apostle Paul to travel tens of thousands of miles on his evangelical journeys, and now Constantine had been appointed to end the persecution of Christians.

AUGUSTINE

The sack of Rome by the Visigoths in 410 posed a severe challenge to Eusebius's interpretation of history. The most famous response was the monumental *De civitate Dei contra paganos* (413–426/427; *City of God*) of St. Augustine of Hippo (354–430). Augustine was forced to confront the argument that the establishment of Christianity as the state religion of Rome had led to the downfall of the empire. His rebuttal dissolved the identity of empire and Christianity. Humanity was composed of two cities, inextricably mixed: the earthly, built on self-love, and the heavenly, animated by the love of God. Only at the Last Judgment would the two be separated. Whatever human glory (or disaster) might attend the earthly city paled in significance compared to the denouement awaiting the heavenly city. Although this vast work (Isidore of Sevilla [c. 560–636] said that anyone who claimed to have read all of it was lying) had great influence, especially in periodizing history, it offered little help to historians who wished to write about the affairs of the earthly city.

The issue of periodization was vital. Augustine divided history into six ages, comparable to the six ages of the individual human life span: from Adam and Eve to the biblical Flood, from the Flood to Abraham, from Abraham to King David, from David to the Babylonian Exile, from the Exile to Jesus, and from Jesus to the Second Coming. Augustine's disciple Paulus Orosius complicated this scheme by introducing apocalyptic material from the Book of Daniel, which was construed as prophesying four kingdoms, the last of which was the Roman Empire. The end of this kingdom would be the end of the world.

St. Mark, illuminated manuscript page from the Gospel Book of the Court school of Charlemagne, c. 810; in the Statsbibliothek, Trier, Ger.

CHRONICLES AND HAGIOGRAPHIES

Although St. Gregory of Tours (538/539–594) and St. Bede the Venerable (672/673–735) wrote histories, early medieval historiography typically took one of two other forms: chronicles and hagiographies, or

EARLY GERMANIC AND ENGLISH HISTORIES

The fall of the Roman Empire actually resulted from the successful attempt of Germanic peoples to occupy its lands and enjoy its benefits. Goths, Lombards, Franks, and other Germanic peoples carved out new kingdoms from the moribund Western empire and adopted its traditions and even its identity. Yet there were difficulties in fitting the Germanic invaders into this pattern. They were nonliterate and preserved their memories of the past orally in heroic poems such as *Beowulf*. Historical writing was almost all done by clerics, in Latin. Gregory of Tours, for example, wrote *Ten Books of Histories*, a history of the Franks from the perspective of the old Gallo-Roman aristocracy, and Bede the Venerable composed the *Historia ecclesiastica gentis Anglorum* (*Ecclesiastical History of the English People*). For both authors, the invaders, once converted to orthodox (Roman) Christianity, were instrumental in repressing heresy: the Franks opposed Arianism (which held that Christ was not divine but created), and the Anglo-Saxons suppressed the irregular practices of the Celtic church.

lives of saints. The spare nature of the earliest chronicles is illustrated by the following excerpt from the chronicle of St. Gall monastery in Switzerland:

- 720 Charles fought against the Saxons.
- 721 Theudo drove the Saxons out of Aquitaine.
- 722 Great crops.
- 723 724 No entries.
- 725 Saracens came for the first time.
- 726 727 728 729 730 No entries.
- 731 Blessed Bede, the presbyter, died.
- 732 Charles fought against the Saracens at Poitiers on Saturday.

Even this rudimentary example, however, exhibits typical characteristics of early medieval chronicles. Only events—human deeds and natural prodigies—are listed. There is no effort to show any causal relationship between them—its style is what rhetoricians call "paratactic" (typically, clauses are simply connected by "and") rather than "hypotactic" (when subordinate conjunctions such as "since" or "therefore" show some sort of relationship between clauses). Although history is presented only in terms of human actions, the absence of causal language makes agency appear limited. Bizarre occurrences in nature are included merely as oddities. For the early medieval chroniclers, the cosmos was bound up in a network of resemblances: bestiaries praised animals for their quasi-human virtues (e.g., bees for industry) and plants owed healing powers to their likeness to parts of the body (walnuts were eaten for disorders of the brain). It was therefore significant when fountains oozed blood or clouds assumed symbolic shapes, since they were indications of the divine will.

Chronicles became richer in the later Middle Ages. They proved to be invaluable resources to later historians, especially in cases in which the chronicler had personal knowledge of the events recorded. The Greater Chronicle of Matthew Paris (died 1259) marks the culmination of the chronicle tradition. Indeed, it seemed so comprehensive that virtually all subsequent English chroniclers confined themselves to copying it. Paris made only one trip outside England and spent most of his time in the monastery of St. Albans. Yet he was well-informed about Western European as well as English history. He seems to have acquired this knowledge partly through his access to a vast number of previous chronicles and state papers and partly through his interaction with the many visitors who stayed at the monastery, including friars who had traveled on the continent. Paris combined his comprehensive knowledge with a lively writing style, which was modeled in some ways on classical historians (for example, he used invented speeches).

Reporting what actually happened was not necessarily the primary goal of even the best chroniclers. Emulation or imitation was valued, and criticism of sources was usually subordinated to copying. Nevertheless, changes in consciousness gradually developed as the Middle Ages wore on. Hagiographies increasingly began to resemble modern biographies, as their writers took more interest in the individuality and development of their characters. The chronicle form disappeared in the 15th century.

As chroniclers recognized human actions, rather than impersonal forces, as the stuff of history, it is not surprising that biography flourished, especially hagiography, or saints' lives. The genre conventionally included details of the saint's childhood, the miracles he performed, and his eventual martyrdom. Understanding of individual character was much less important than the moral lessons and encouragement conveyed by the story.

NEW FORMS

Two writers who in very different ways pointed to new forms of historiography were Otto of Freising (c. 1111–58) and Geoffrey of Villehardouin (c. 1150–c. 1213). Otto, the uncle of the emperor Frederick Barbarossa, had received the best education available in his time, which meant studying dialectic and theology in Paris (perhaps under the theologian and philosopher Peter Abelard). Because history was not regularly taught in medieval schools or universities, it is not surprising that Otto adopted a more philosophical approach in his *Chronica sive historia de duabus civitatibus* (*Chronicle or History of the Two Cities*). As its title indicates, the work was inspired by Augustine. Beginning, as many chronicles did, with the Creation and ending in 1146, it reflects abundantly on the miseries of "wars and tottering kingdoms." Otto, like Orosius, identified the City of God with the church. Yet the "Chronicle" deals with ecclesiastical affairs with remarkable objectivity, considering Otto's kinship with the German emperors. He describes the Investiture Controversy between the German ruler Henry IV and Pope Gregory VII and states arguments both for and against the so-called Donation of Constantine (an 8th-century forgery that came to be the basis for papal claims to temporal power). Although he prudently avoids giving unnecessary offense, he defends writing that might anger his predecessors, because "it is better to fall into the hands of men than to abandon the function of a historian by covering up a loathsome sight by colours that conceal the truth."

Otto participated in the Second Crusade (1146–48) but did not write about it. The Crusades raised interpretative problems that historians had not faced before. Because nothing like the Crusades had ever happened, they posed new issues of historical causality. They brought Europeans into massive—though not invariably hostile—contact with Islamic civilization, and they inspired new kinds of historical writing. Villehardouin, a French nobleman and military commander, was an eyewitness of the Fourth Crusade (1201–04). His *Conquête de Constantinople* (*The Conquest of Constantinople*) was the first sustained work of French prose and one of the first great memoirs in French.

Precisely because Villehardouin did not know how histories "ought" to be written, however, his work lacked the conventional preface modestly declaring the author's lack of ability. His history is basically the memoir of a successful commander. It is free of the moral reflections beloved of monks and the rhetorical effusions indulged in by emulators of the Latin

ISLAMIC HISTORIOGRAPHY

The Qur'ān, the sacred text of Islam, contains allusions that constitute the basis of a providential history of humankind from Adam through Muhammad, the founder of Islam. Another valuable resource for Islamic historians is the Hadith (the traditions or sayings of Muhammad), which is arranged in such a way that lines of transmission can be traced back to those who knew the Prophet. Chains of authorities were thus integral to early Islamic theology and historiography, which naturally lent themselves to annalistic treatment.

The greatest early Islamic historian, al-Ṭabarī (839–923), was reputed to have memorized the Qur'ān at the age of seven. Legend credited him with producing a 30,000-page commentary on the Qur'ān and an equally long universal history (both survive but are only one-tenth as long). His chief virtues as a historian were his accurate chronology and his scrupulous faithfulness in reproducing authorities. Like Christian annalists, he depended on the Hebrew Bible (as interpreted by Islam), though the world he inhabited was basically Egypt and Muslim Asia rather than Western Christendom. The Persian scholar Rashīd al-Dīn (1247–1318) composed a more truly universal history, "Jāmi' al-tawārīkh" ("Collector of Chronicles"), which covered not only the Islamic world (which by then extended from Spain to northern India) but also included data on the popes and emperors of Europe and on Mongolia and China.

The sophistication of Islamic historical thought was dramatically illustrated by the *Muqaddimah* ("Introduction") of the Arab historian Ibn Khaldūn (1332–1406). This introductory volume of a universal history reveals Khaldūn's ideas about

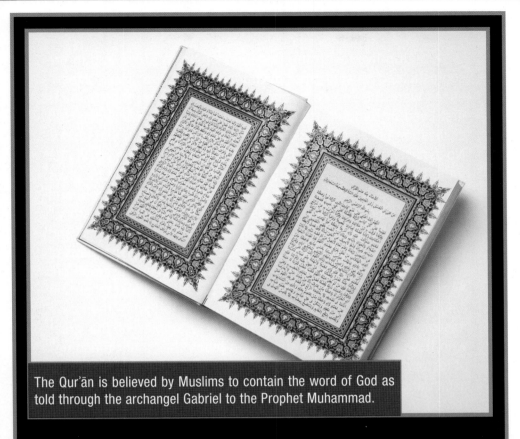

The Qur'ān is believed by Muslims to contain the word of God as told through the archangel Gabriel to the Prophet Muhammad.

history—something chroniclers hardly ever did. The subjects Khaldūn considered in his work include historical method, geography, culture, economics, public finance, population, society and state, religion and politics, and the social context of knowledge. Khaldūn held high office and was often exiled or imprisoned. Late in his life he had the opportunity to discuss history with the Mongol emperor Timur the Lame, who was besieging Damascus. Timur wrote his own memoirs, and he was evidently interested not only in what Khaldūn knew about North Africa but also in his philosophy of history.

Continued on page 24

Continued from page 23

Khaldūn lived with the Bedouins of North Africa and in the sophisticated Muslim cities of Granada and Cairo. These experiences were the source of one of his main ideas: that humans first lived in Bedouin tribes and then achieved civilization, but civilization became decadent with increasing wealth and luxury. No dynasty or civilization, he believed, could maintain vitality for more than four generations (though the only example he gives is the decline of the Israelites after Abraham, Isaac, Jacob, and Joseph). Khaldūn contrasted his writing with "surface history," which was "no more than information about political events" and was used to "entertain large, crowded gatherings." Historians of his day, he thought, were too credulous in accepting tradition. As for their frequent moralizing about the misconduct of certain caliphs, Khaldūn asserted that people like to justify their own misconduct by looking in histories for examples of the great who have done the same things. To reach the "inner meaning" of history, the historian had to be "speculative" and give "subtle explanations" of causes. To accomplish this, history had to be rooted in philosophy—or, as Khaldūn said of his own work, it had to be a new and original science.

historians. With Villehardouin a new voice—vivacious, conventionally pious but impatient of theological niceties, and keenly interested in military and political strategies—entered historical discourse.

HISTORY IN THE RENAISSANCE

In the 12th century, Europeans took an avid interest in the Arabic translations and commentaries on Greek medical, mathematical, and, especially, philosophical works. By the time of Ibn Khaldūn (1332–1406), this interest had waned, and his work would influence only later European historians. The idea of history as a new science, however, would have a long career, beginning with some historians of the Renaissance.

The nature, origins, and even existence of the Renaissance has been subject to intensive investigation since the early 20th century. The term has been applied to cultural movements in the 9th and 12th centuries, and medieval precedents have been identified for developments that were previously thought to be unique to the Renaissance. This is as true for historiography as for any other aspect of Renaissance culture; but while the differences between the Renaissance and the earlier Middle Ages may have been exaggerated, they do exist. Nobody could mistake a historian such as Niccolò Machiavelli (1469–1527) for Matthew Paris (died 1259).

PETRARCH

Although he was not exactly a historian, the Italian scholar and poet Petrarch (1304–74) illustrates much that was distinctive about the Renaissance attitude toward history. If not the first to coin the term *Middle Ages,* he consistently held that his own age (subsequently to be called the Renaissance) had made a decisive break with the 10 centuries that followed the decline of the Roman Empire. His true contemporaries, he thought, were the historians and poets of Rome's Golden Age (c. 70 BCE–18 CE), to whom he addressed a series of letters, "Epistolae metricae" (begun 1350). The letter to Livy expresses Plutarch's wish that he had been born in Livy's time or Livy in his; thanks him for transporting Petrarch into the company of the worthies of ancient Rome instead of "the thievish company of today among whom I was born under an evil star"; and concludes: "Farewell forever, matchless historian!…Written… in the thirteen hundred and fiftieth year from the birth of Him whom you would have seen, or of whose birth you could have heard, had you lived a little longer."

In general, medieval historians had little understanding of the radical differences between their society and that of the Romans. Petrarch had an appreciation of the discontinuity between past and present, however, as well as a painful sense of his own anachronism. For him, all aspects of a culture were constantly changing. Petrarch also exhibited an antiquarian interest that would eventually enrich the study of history.

LORENZO VALLA

Renaissance humanists were above all philologists, rhetoricians, and editors and emulators of the texts of Latin (and later Greek) antiquity. One of their triumphs was the demonstration by Lorenzo Valla (1407–57) that the so-called Donation of Constantine could not have been authentic. This document had been suspect, on various grounds, for centuries; Valla's argument was distinguished by his proof that its Latin style and diction belonged to the 8th century and not the 4th. With similar philological arguments Petrarch discredited a charter exempting Austria from imperial jurisdiction. Two other famous documents, the Isidorian Decretals (also known as the False Decretals) and the writings of Dionysius the Areopagite, eventually earned the prefix pseudo through Renaissance scholarship.

FLAVIO BIONDO AND LEONARDO BRUNI

Antiquarians such as Petrarch were interested in all sorts of relics of the past, material objects as well as texts—an interest that eventually led to social and economic history and even to "everyday history" and "history from below." In his works on Roman antiquities Flavio Biondo (1392–1463) virtually founded the field of archaeology. His *Historiarum ab inclinatione Romanorum imperii decades* ("Decades of History from the Deterioration of the Roman Empire"), for example, introduced the concept of the decline of the Roman Empire and the idea of the Middle Ages as the period from 410 to 1410. In addition, he used the new textual criticism to eliminate many legends that had been accepted as facts in previous histories.

Biondo, however, was not what his contemporaries called a "pure historian." The model of pure history was the *Historiarum Florentini populi libri XII* ("Twelve Books of Histories of the Florentine People"), by Leonardo Bruni (c. 1370–1444). Although Bruni owed much to the chronicles kept by the Italian cities, he drew extensively from ancient historians and, having learned Greek, was one of the first Europeans since ancient times to read Thucydides. Bruni was greatly influenced by Livy, who provided the paradigmatic account of how a city is founded and becomes great. Bruni scrupulously (though not slavishly) followed Livy's example in his emphasis on politics—he found nothing worth relating for the year 1348, when the Black Death first struck Florence—and on individual character as the cause of historical actions. He also restricted himself to the vocabulary that Livy used or could have used.

Bruni's central theme was the people of Florence. His history followed a strong narrative line that described the rise to power of the Florentines and their victory in their war against Milan, which Bruni believed was made possible by republican virtue, or civic humanism. That same pride continued to animate other Florentine historians, even the apparently cynical Machiavelli.

NICCOLÒ MACHIAVELLI

Whereas Bruni had written at the apex of Florentine power, Machiavelli's public career was marked by the desperate situation created by what he called "the calamity": the invasion of Italy first by the French in 1494 and later by the imperial forces of Charles V in 1527. As a diplomat and later secretary to Florence's ruling Council of Ten, Machiavelli observed and tried to influence the shifting alliances between the Italian city-states. When the Medici family returned to power and ousted him from office, he turned to reflections on politics and history. In addition to *Il principe* (1532; *The Prince*), his most famous work, he wrote the *Discorsi sopra la prima deca di Tito Livio* (1531; *Discourses on Livy*), the *Istorie Fiorentine* (1532; *Florentine Histories*), and *Dell'arte della guerra* (1521; *The Art of War*). Machiavelli presented his thoughts on history as "a new route" that would provide instruction to the statesmen of his day by marshaling examples from ancient history. As he writes in the *Discourses on Livy*,

> **Whoever considers the past and the present will readily observe that all cities and all peoples are and ever have been animated by the same desires and the same passions; so that it is easy, by diligent study of the past, to foresee what is likely to happen in the future in any republic, and to apply those remedies that were used by the ancients, or, not finding any that were employed by them, to devise new ones from the similarity of the events.**

History thus would become political science. Machiavelli, however, did not always respect his data in cases in which the historical situation did not lend itself to the maxim of statecraft he was trying to inculcate.

FRANCESCO GUICCIARDINI

Machiavelli's younger contemporary Francesco Guicciardini (1483–1540) shared some of Machiavelli's attitudes but not his rationale for studying history. "It is most fallacious," he wrote, "to judge by examples; because unless these be in all respects parallel they are of no use, the least divergence in the circumstances giving rise to the widest possible divergence in the conclusions." Instead, in his *Storia d'Italia* (1537–40; *History of Italy*), Guicciardini attempted to explain why Italy had been unable to resist foreign incursions. Writing the history of such a diverse area was itself an innovation, for which Guicciardini's diplomatic experience served him well; but he also drew from the repertoire of classical historians the technique of the character, or psychological, sketch of the leading actors. Since Guicciardini, like almost all Renaissance historians, believed that historical change resulted from the *virtù* (or lack of it) of individuals, the ability to draw a brilliant character—at which he excelled—enhanced the explanatory power of his work.

GIORGIO VASARI

It is thus not surprising that biographies flourished in the Renaissance. Some were of individuals, but a more typical genre was multiple biographies. Petrarch, again, was a pioneer with his *De viris illustribus* (begun 1338; *Illustrious Men*). A still more famous example was *Le vite de' più eccellenti architetti, pittori, et scultori* (1550; *Lives of the Most Eminent Painters, Sculptors, and Architects)*, by Giorgio Vasari. Vasari did not simply compile a series of biographical sketches; he grouped them into three periods, which were marked by a progressive improvement in artistic technique. He concluded that "it is inherent in the very nature of these arts to progress step by step from modest beginnings, and finally to reach the summit of perfection." He noted that in his own day "art has achieved everything possible in the imitation of nature, and has progressed so far that it has more reason to fear slipping back than to expect ever to make further advances." This last

Self-portrait by Giorgio Vasari, oil on canvas; in the Uffizi Gallery, Florence

clause hints at the belief in historical cycles which was common in Renaissance thought. Vasari acknowledged that the arts of the ancients had also risen and then declined.

It is easy to make the Renaissance too modern. It was an era in which beliefs in magic and in numerology had wide currency. It is also possible to exaggerate the level of interest in history during this period. Thus, the archetypal "Renaissance man," Leonardo da Vinci, seems to have had little interest in acquiring historical knowledge. Renaissance humanists, however, made positive contributions to the study of history, and the humanist approach to the past helped to create the great upheaval of the Reformation.

CHAPTER THREE

EARLY MODERN, ENLIGHTENMENT, AND ROMANTIC HISTORIOGRAPHY

M artin Luther (1483–1546), the German theologian who set the Reformation in motion, at first glance bears little resemblance to Petrarch, much less to Machiavelli. But while his piety was intense, he embraced much of the new learning. Nobody was more insistent on returning to the sources, which for him meant the New Testament. Any belief or practice not found there, he thought, must be a human invention, introduced during the long period of papal perversion of the Christian faith.

CHURCH HISTORY

Protestantism thus entailed a reinterpretation of church history as well as of the Bible. As a consequence, history, which was not part of the curriculum in medieval universities, came to be taught in Protestant ones. (The early association of history and German universities became important later.)

CENTURIAE MAGDEBURGENSES AND ANNALES ECCLESIASTICI

Luther's followers also set about publishing their version of church history. Ulrich von Hutten (1488–1523) published a manuscript of Valla's

Martin Luther (1483–1546)

treatise on the Donation of Constantine, impudently dedicating it to the pope. A team of scholars (a novelty) toured Germany, Denmark, Scotland, and Austria looking for documents on which to base their *Centuriae Magdeburgenses* (1559–75; *Magdeburg Centuries*), a 13-volume work that constituted a denunciation of the course of church history up to 1300. The *Centuriae Magdeburgenses* was in some ways regressive; the compilers could not think of any more satisfactory arrangement for their material than by centuries, and their credulity toward documents damaging to the papacy was as invariable as the critical acumen they deployed to discredit every basis of papal authority. Nevertheless, they unearthed large quantities of data. The *Centuriae Magdeburgenses* called forth an equally voluminous and tendentious Roman Catholic response, the *Annales Ecclesiastici* (*Ecclesiastical Annals*), by Caesar Baronius (1538–1607), also in 13 volumes and also organized by centuries. This in turn was refuted by Isaac Casaubon (1559–1614), who was outraged that Baronius had attempted to write ecclesiastical history without knowing either ancient Greek or Hebrew.

PAOLO SARPI

One great work that emerged from this era of often tedious controversy was Paolo Sarpi's *Istoria del Concilio Tridentino* (1619; *History of the Council of Trent*). Sarpi, whose range of interests and accomplishments rivaled those of da Vinci, knew Greek and Hebrew and was able to do extensive historical research and to mold the results into a compelling literary form. Sarpi was a friar and, by his lights, a loyal Catholic, but he was also a loyal Venetian and hence an opponent of the temporal powers of the pope. He understood that the Council of Trent (1545–63) had quashed the last hope of reuniting Christendom. In its attack on the Jesuits, the guardians of Roman Catholic theological orthodoxy, the *History* demonstrated a mastery of irony, sarcasm, and ridicule that was not approached again until *Les Provinciales*, by the French mathematician and philosopher Blaise Pascal (1623–62).

Despite its errors and biases, it remains a masterpiece of Italian prose. And, like the controversy between Baronius and the authors of the *Centuriae Magdeburgenses*, it stimulated the publication of many additional sources for the study of medieval history.

Sarpi's work closed an epoch in Italian historiography. In the late 16th and 17th centuries France became the centre of historiographical innovation, which was applied now to the history of law. This field became almost as contentious as the history of religion but was ultimately more fruitful, since it opened lines of inquiry that eventually led to modern conceptions of history.

LEGAL HISTORY

France was the earliest beneficiary of the rise of Italian humanistic scholarship, but it differed from Italy in ways that facilitated fruitful extension of the new learning. The Protestant stimulus to historiography was much stronger in France, and there was also no inquisition or *Index Librorum Prohibitorum* (Latin: "Index of Prohibited Books") to suppress free inquiry. Whereas Italian humanists tended to regard the Middle Ages as an embarrassing interlude between the glories of ancient Rome and their own time, France had been the intellectual centre of Europe during that period. Furthermore, any serious treatment of medieval history required sorting out Germanic elements from Roman ones, a problem that the French were better able to undertake.

GUILLAUME BUDÉ AND FRANÇOIS HOTMAN

Throughout the Middle Ages the Code of Justinian, or *Corpus Juris Civilis* ("Body of Civil Law"), the four-volume codification of Roman law compiled under the patronage of the Byzantine emperor Justinian

(483–565), was regarded as the quintessence of human law, applicable in virtually every situation. Parts of it were contradictory or barely intelligible, but commentators regarded these difficulties as the result of their own hermeneutic ineptitude. In the 15th century, however, humanists (among them Lorenzo Valla) assumed instead that the text had been corrupted by its compilers and that its pure form could be recovered through the application of philological methods. In France, Guillaume Budé (1467–1540) followed Valla's example, and his commentary on the Pandects, the second volume of Justinian's code, established the power of this approach. Budé's commentary and his book on the economic history of the Roman Empire earned him a scholarly prestige comparable to that of the great Dutch humanist Erasmus.

The effort to recover the pure text of Justinian's code required both sensitivity to linguistic change and the ability to establish the historical context in which the Pandects were compiled. These became the hallmarks of the so-called "French mode" of legal studies, which ousted the unhistorical "Italian mode" from most French universities within a single generation. The more radical implications of the French approach, however, remained to be revealed. If the Code of Justinian was a jumble of republican and imperial law, as the French school held, then, as François Hotman (1524–90) concluded, the laws of Rome were irrelevant to those of France. This conclusion was of more than antiquarian import, since Hotman attributed tendencies toward absolutism in the French monarchy to the influence of Roman law; the monarchy of the Franks, in his view, was more limited.

FRANÇOIS BAUDOUIN AND JEAN BODIN

Although the new study of law was closely related to historiography, the early commentaries on civil law did not constitute histories. The two disciplines were married in theory in *Institution of Universal History and Its*

Connection with Jurisprudence by François Baudouin (1520–73) and the *Method for the Easy Understanding of History* by Jean Bodin (1530–96). These two works belonged to an extremely popular genre, the *ars historica* ("art of history"). Baudouin's work, though repeating all the old commonplaces about the virtues of history, was also a handbook—perhaps the first—of historical method. Acknowledging that rhetoric is history's mother and political science its sister, Baudouin declared that history ought to narrate and explain historical events themselves, as well as their causes and consequences. To establish historical truth, the historian should rely on eyewitness accounts, or, lacking these, primary sources. Although history was partly geographic in scope, it required also, in principle, attention to all human culture (for Baudouin this meant ecclesiastical as well as political and military history).

Bodin's book shared many of Baudouin's ideas. Although Bodin placed history "above all sciences," he actually wished to extract from it the materials for a transcendent political philosophy and a universal jurisprudence. He attempted this in *Les Six Livres de la République* (1576; *The Six Books of the Commonwealth*).

ÉTIENNE PASQUIER

The union of historiographical theory and practice was best achieved by Étienne Pasquier (1529–1615) in his *Recherches de la France* (1560–1621), which may be regarded as the first work of modern history. Pasquier denied that medieval chronicles were "authorities," instead regarding them as raw materials or primary sources, no more credible than law codes or even folk traditions. Medieval French chronicles usually began the story of the French people by tracing their descent from some hero of the Trojan War. Although these stories had lost credibility, no convincing alternative had been developed. Pasquier began his story with the Gauls, and, since the chronicles said almost nothing about them, he reconstructed their history from comments in Julius Caesar's *De bello Gallico* (*Gallic Wars*). He read Caesar just as critically as any chronicle, however, reversing the Roman leader's negative value judgments where appropriate and wringing from the texts a picture that Caesar supplies almost in spite of himself.

Pasquier's ability to recognize and utilize the best historical sources available is also demonstrated in his treatment of Joan of Arc, the peasant who led French armies against the English during the Hundred Years' War. Not yet an enormous cult figure, Joan was treated in many chronicles as an intriguer and impostor or, even worse, a witch or heretic. Yet the records of her trial, which allow her to speak in her own voice, were accessible, as were those of the second trial, which rehabilitated her character and quashed the accusations that led to her execution. Not only did Pasquier base his account

Joan of Arc at the Coronation of Charles VII in Reims Cathedral, oil on canvas by J.-A.-D. Ingres, 1854; in the Louvre Museum, Paris. 240 x 178 cm.

squarely on these primary sources, he also incorporated crucial sections of these documents into his text. This practice of quoting documents to support historians' claims, universal today, was controversial at the time. The classical model discouraged quoting other writers (hence the use of invented speech).

THE BOLLANDIST FATHERS AND JEAN MABILLON

Progress in historiography is hard to establish, and there are clear cases of regress. In 17th-century France the discredited story of Trojan origins returned. Scholars in the 16th century, while not denying that God's will might be the ultimate cause of everything, had focused entirely on secondary causes; in the following century, however, the most influential historical work was *Discours sur l'histoire universelle* (1681; *Discourse on Universal History*), by the French bishop Jacques-Bénigne Bossuet, which restored a providential interpretation of history.

Despite these developments, scholarly advances occurred in the study of history, most notably those made by clergymen studying medieval charters and the lives of the saints. A group of Jesuits who came to be known as the Bollandist Fathers compiled biographies of all the saints in the calendar of the Roman church—a collective task that has continued into the 21st century. The Bollandists' scrupulously high standards of evidence and analysis has resulted in the removal from the calendar of a number of saints who had the misfortune not to have existed.

Using the results of their researches, the Bollandists challenged the authenticity of many of the charters of the Benedictine houses in France. Some of these documents were certainly forgeries, and the danger of forfeiture of the houses naturally created a demand for a method of authenticating charters. This need was met by a Benedictine of St. Maur, Jean Mabillon (1632–1707), in his *De re diplomatica* (1681), which can be regarded as the founding work of diplomatics, or the study of charters. Mabillon's methodology was comprehensive—he examined ink, parchment, and handwriting style and compared one charter with others. Indeed, he did his work so well that little has since been added to it.

In light of the tendentious histories of this turbulent period, the intellectual honesty and modesty of the Bollandists is refreshing. One of them wrote to Mabillon, after reading his treatise:

> **"I have no other satisfaction in having written upon the subject than that of having given occasion for the writing of a treatise so masterly. It is true that I felt at first some pain in reading your book, where I saw myself refuted in so unanswerable a manner; but finally…seeing the truth in its clearest light, I invited my companion to come and share the admiration with which I felt myself filled."**

ENLIGHTENMENT HISTORIOGRAPHY: SCIENCE AND SKEPTICISM

Two new challenges confronted the study of history in the 17th century. One was generated by the successes of natural science, claimed by its proponents to be the best—or even the only—producer of truth. Science created a new picture of the world, discrediting all past conceptions. As the English poet Alexander Pope wrote: "Nature and nature's laws lay hid in night / Then God said: 'Let Newton be!' and all was light." These successes inspired the hope that similar laws would be found for social and historical phenomena and that the same scientific methods could be applied to every subject, including politics, economics, and even literature.

The other challenge lay in the relativism and skepticism generated within historical discourse itself. In his *Histoire des histoires et l'idée de l'histoire accompli* (1599; *History of Histories and the Idea of History Accomplished*), Lancelot Voisin La Popelinière (1540–1608) asked: if history shows the ceaseless mutations of human culture, what keeps history

René Descartes (1596–1650)

itself from being more than a mode of perception of any particular culture, of no more permanent value than any other changeable cultural artifact? Thus, the unmasking of forgeries could lead to suspicions about every relic of the past. In a similar vein, the French Jesuit Jean Hardouin claimed that almost all the Latin and Greek classics and most of the works of the Church Fathers, including St. Augustine and St. Jerome, were written by a group of medieval Italian scholars, who then forged all the manuscripts purporting to be earlier. Hardouin, it must be said, pushed historical criticism past the boundaries of sanity.

The most influential philosopher of the 17th century, René Descartes, included history in his catalogue of dubious sciences. In his *Discourse on Method* (1637), Descartes asserted that, although histories exalt the mind,

> **even the most accurate of histories, if they do not exactly misrepresent or exaggerate the value of things in order to render them more worthy of being read, at least omit in them all the circumstances which are basest and least notable; and from this it follows that what is retained is not portrayed as it really is, and that those who regulate their conduct by examples which they derive from such a source are liable to fall into the extravagances of the knights-errant of romances.**

According to Descartes, history is doubtful because it is selective. Unlike the sciences, which are based on mathematics, history cannot yield knowledge.

One attempt to rescue the truth-claims of history, which ironically lent support to skepticism, was the *Dictionnaire historique et critique* (1697; *Historical and Critical Dictionary*), by the French philosopher Pierre Bayle (1647–1706), one of the most widely read works of the 18th century. The articles in Bayle's dictionary, enlivened by learned and often witty marginalia, established what was known about the subject but often undermined religious and political orthodoxies. These sallies were far more memorable than the often trivial facts provided in the work.

MONTESQUIEU AND VOLTAIRE

The leading historians of the French Enlightenment, Montesquieu (1689–1755) and Voltaire (1694–1778), responded in different ways to the scientific impulse. In *De l'esprit des loix* (1748; *The Spirit of Laws*), Montesquieu explored the natural order that he believed underlay polities as well as economies. Despite lacking information about many cultures, he systematically applied a comparative method of analysis. Climate and soil, he believed, are the deepest level of causality. The size of the territory to be governed also determines what kind of government it can have (republics have to be small; large countries like Russia require despotism). Montesquieu's preferred form of government was constitutional monarchy, which existed in France before Louis XIV (reigned 1643–1715) and in England during Montesquieu's day. Among his many readers were the Founding Fathers of the United States, who embraced Montesquieu's idea of balanced government and indeed created one exquisitely contrived to allow each branch to check the others.

Voltaire's temperament was more skeptical. "History," he declared, "is a pack of tricks we play on the dead." He nevertheless spent much of his life playing those tricks, producing *L'Histoire de Charles XII* (1731; *History of Charles XII*), on the Swedish monarch, *Le Siècle de Louis XIV* (1751; *The Century of Louis XIV*), and *Essai sur les moeurs* (1756; *Essay on Morals*). In an article on history for the *Encyclopédie*, edited by the philosopher Denis Diderot, Voltaire noted that the modern historian requires not only precise facts and dates but also attention to customs, commerce, finance, agriculture, and population. This was the program that the *Essai* tried to fulfill. It starts not with Adam or the Greek poet Homer but with the ancient Chinese, and it also treats Indian, Persian, and Arab civilizations. Voltaire's *Essai* was the first attempt to make the genre of "universal history" truly universal, not just in covering the globe—or at least the high cultures—but also in studying every aspect of human life. In this respect Voltaire is the father of the "total histories" and the "histories of everyday life" that blossomed in the second half of the 20th century.

Voltaire was curious about everything—but not tolerant of everything. Like most philosophes (the leading thinkers of the French Enlightenment), he considered the Middle Ages an epoch of unbroken superstition and barbarism. Even the age of Louis XIV exhibited "a history of human stupidity." Like Machiavelli, he believed that one could learn from history—but only what not to do. Thus, a statesman reading a history of the reign of Charles XII should be "cured of the folly of war."

Although Voltaire was interested in other cultures, he believed that reason had made headway only in the Europe of his own day. It was left to thinkers of the next generation, including the baron l'Aulne Turgot (1727–81) and the marquis de Condorcet (1743–94), to construe history as gradually but inevitably moving toward the elimination of bigotry, superstition, and ignorance. Condorcet rhapsodized: "How welcome to the philosopher is this picture of the human race, freed from all its chains, released from the domination of chance and from that of the enemies of progress, advancing with a firm and sure step on the path of truth, virtue, and happiness."

EDWARD GIBBON

Science contributed not only its ambitions but also its concepts to historiography. The philosopher David Hume (1711–76) took from it the sober empiricism and distrust of grand schemes that informed his *History of England* (1754–62). The greatest of the Enlightenment historians— and probably the only one still read today—Edward Gibbon (1737–94), managed to bring together in *The Decline and Fall of the Roman Empire* (1776–88) the erudition of the 17th century and the philosophy of the 18th. Gibbon borrowed rather than contributed to historical erudition, for he was not a great archival researcher. "It would be unreasonable," he said, "to expect that the historian should peruse enormous volumes,

Edward Gibbon, oil painting by Henry Walton, 1774; in the National Portrait Gallery, London

with the uncertain hope of extracting a few interesting lines." The influence of Enlightenment thought is indicated particularly in Gibbon's wit and in his skeptical view of religion. "To the believer," he wrote, "all religions are equally true, to the philosopher, all religions are equally false, and to the magistrate, all religions are equally useful."

Gibbon's great work gives no elaborate account of the causes of the decline and fall—because the causes, he thought, were obvious. Borrowing an image from physics, he wrote:

> **the decline of Rome was the natural and inevitable effect of immoderate greatness. Prosperity ripened the principle of decay; the causes of destruction multiplied with the extent of conquest; and as soon as time or accident had removed the artificial supports, the stupendous fabric yielded to the pressure of its own weight. The story of its ruin is simple and obvious; and instead of enquiring why the Roman Empire was destroyed, we should rather be surprised that it had subsisted so long.**

The Enlightenment has been condemned as "unhistorical." It did lack sympathy, and thus full understanding, of some cultures and periods. Hume's view that human nature was essentially the same in the Roman Empire and in 18th-century Britain now seems wrong. No technical advances in historiography were made by the philosophes. On the other hand, history was widely read, and the brilliant writing of Voltaire and Gibbon helped to create something like a mass public for historical works. Finally, the Enlightenment expanded the historical world, in principle at least, almost to the limits recognized today—and it never shrank again.

HISTORIOGRAPHY IN ENGLAND

Romanticism crossed the English Channel, though naturally with variations, and it also crossed the Atlantic Ocean. Thomas Babington Macaulay (1800–59) proclaimed that the central theme of English history from the time of the granting of the Magna Carta in 1215 to his own day involved the gradual increase of liberty. His *History of England from the Accession of James II* (1849–61) situated the genius of the English in achieving liberty by largely peaceful means, thus sparing himself the task of accounting for England's medieval regicides or the English Civil Wars. The English had enough respect for the past to avoid violent change but enough flexibility to avoid rigid conservatism. In the first volume, Macaulay wrote a classic description of English life in 1685. His picture of England was highly pleasing to 19th-century Victorians, who bought hundreds of thousands of copies.

More directly influenced by Romanticism, as by German thought, was Thomas Carlyle. To him, Macaulay's views, besides being complacent, were insipid. Conflicts between peoples and the actions of great men were the stuff of history. "Universal History," he declared in *On Heroes, Hero-Worship, and the Heroic in History* (1841), "... is at bottom the History of the Great Men who have worked here. They were the leaders of men, these great ones," and history was "the essence of innumerable biographies."

The works of many Romantic historians were notable for their literary style. More people, however, derived their sense of the past from the historical novels of Sir Walter Scott (1771–1832). Ranke's career as a modern historian began when he discovered factual errors in Scott's novels; Scott was also Marx's favourite novelist. The emphasis the Romantics put on imagination in recreating the past opened the way for the genre of historical novels, of which Scott was the first great practitioner.

ROMANTIC HISTORIOGRAPHY

Nevertheless, it is hard to see how historiography could have developed further within the limits established by the Enlightenment worldview. A second generation of philosophes, especially the philosopher Jean-Jacques Rousseau, were already testing those limits in the later 18th century; but the most potent challenge to them came from Germany, now finally assuming its full place in the intellectual life of Europe. The period 1770–1830 witnessed the activity of an astonishing constellation of German thinkers, poets, and eventually historians, of whom Johann Wolfgang von Goethe, Immanuel Kant, Friedrich von Schiller, and Georg Wilhelm Friedrich Hegel are only the best known.

JOHANN GOTTFRIED VON HERDER

Perhaps even more influential than these figures, however, was Johann Gottfried von Herder (1744–1803). Herder was a polymath—as much a theologian, philosopher, anthropologist, or literary critic as a theorist of history. His *Ideen zur Philosophie der Geschichte der Menscheit* (1784–91; *Outlines of a Philosophy of the History of Man*) anticipated Darwin in its claim that all organic life is connected and evolving progressively toward human beings, the highest form of life.

Herder held a tripartite view of historical development and was interested in what he conceived as the spirit of cultures. He posited an age of primitive human poets whose consciousness was distilled in epics. An age of prose followed as humans became mature, but it was only in the "ripe" age—inevitably metaphorically associated with senescence—that language became precise enough to be suitable for philosophical reflection.

The same preoccupation with language underlies Herder's thoughts about culture—or *Volk*, as he called it. Within a culture's language, he wrote, "dwell its entire world of tradition, history, religion, principles of existence: its whole heart and soul." The language of a *Volk* is created in its youth or poetic age; afterward it is relatively resistant to changes imposed from the outside. Herder resisted the notion that any age or Volk is inferior to any other.

It is not hard to detect a German declaration of independence in these views. "Germany," after all, was a cultural but not a political unity. The exaltation of all cultures as equal and the admiration for "primitive" humans stood in contrast to French cultural chauvinism and the grading of people according to how closely they reached the Enlightenment standard of rationality. Furthermore, Herder turned the interests of historians away from political and diplomatic history and toward social, cultural, and intellectual history.

Even more profoundly, Herder elevated the historical imagination to supreme importance. This did not mean that he favoured fantasy, the invention of speeches, or other deliberate falsifications. But he thought that the spiritual development of a people cannot be discerned by purely rational processes. The ways in which the art of a people, for example, is related to its economic or social institutions has to be grasped in an act of insight. An impressionistic thinker, Herder sensed the aspects of the Enlightenment that his generation found unsatisfying. He is generally regarded as the father of Romanticism.

GIAMBATTISTA VICO

During the Romantic movements, thinkers reevaluated past thought and looked for what might be usable in it. This process led to the discovery by the French historian Jules Michelet (1798–1874) of the eccentric *Scienza nuova* (1725; *New Science*) of the Neapolitan professor of rhetoric Giambattista Vico (1688–1744). Much of the *Scienza nuova* deals with problems in the history of Roman law (which had preoccupied 16th- and 17th-century scholars), but it also proposes a new methodology for history, a scheme of how it develops, and a reformulation of the providential theory.

In opposition to the philosophy of Descartes, Vico argued that only history can produce certainty. According to Vico, humans can have knowledge of "the world of nations" because they created it, but only God can know the natural world. The English philosopher Thomas Hobbes had equated *verum* ("truth") and *factum* ("the made"), but Vico made this a fundamental principle of historiography, one that he hoped would make it the queen of the sciences.

One problem for Vico, which he says took him many years of effort to solve, was that of the nature of primitive mentality. In opposition to "the conceit of scholars"—the assumption that primitive humans must have had worldviews and mental processes like those of the Enlightenment—Vico held that the authors of the *Iliad*, the ancient Greek poem attributed to Homer, were individuals of powerful imaginations who could express themselves only through poetic metaphors. Among these metaphors was Zeus, the god who throws down thunderbolts, and his equivalent in every other gentile culture. This age of gods was succeeded by an age of heroes and finally by an age of men, whose characteristic expression was prose and whose inevitable trope was irony.

HISTORIOGRAPHY IN THE UNITED STATES

The most influential American historian of the 19th century was George Bancroft (1800–91), who studied at the universities of Göttingen and Berlin. During intervals in a busy career as a public official he wrote a 10-volume *History of the United States* (1834–74), which placed the country within God's plan for all humanity. The European colonists who settled the country brought with them the "vital principles of Teutonic liberty." With the signing of the Declaration of Independence, "a new plebeian democracy took its place by the side of the proudest empire," a democracy that was destined to spread the blessings of liberty to the rest of the world. As to spreading the blessings of liberty to American slaves, Bancroft argued that slavery was imposed on the United States and that it played a role in the providential plan. The resonance within his work not only of Romantic principles (it can be seen as an adaptation of Hegel) but also American political rhetoric of the 19th century explains its wide appeal.

Other American historians, such as Francis Parkman (1823–93), William Prescott (1796–1859), and John Lothrop Motley (1814–77), also addressed epic themes in captivating language. Parkman's theme was the contest between France, Britain, and the Native Americans for possession of North America. Prescott and Motley recounted the wars of imperial Spain in the Golden Age of the 16th and 17th centuries. Prescott's theme was the conquest of Mexico and Peru; Motley (also a product of Göttingen and Berlin) recounted the successful rebellion of the Netherlands, which he did not fail to compare frequently to the American Revolution.

GEORG WILHELM FRIEDRICH HEGEL

Vico and Herder worked toward a conception of "spirit of the times" and "spirit of the people," both of which were incorporated into Hegel's enormously ambitious philosophy of history. Hegel's thought eludes easy summation, and its premises are not intuitively obvious. As an absolute idealist, he held that only ideas are real (in Hegel's famous phrase, "the real is rational"). Ideas develop by contradiction, or by implying their opposites, since establishing what a concept is involves determining what it is not. Thus, pure being implies not-being; but since it is pure being, it is not anything in particular, and hence it is also a kind of nothingness. From the ideas of pure being and nothingness the idea of becoming is inevitably generated. This is one example of what is usually called (though seldom by Hegel) dialectic. The Idea, or Spirit, for Hegel must realize itself by being incarnated in the world—in inorganic, animal, and vegetable life because they obey natural laws, and in human history because "World history in general is the development of Spirit in Time, just as Nature is the development of the Idea in Space."

The goal toward which Spirit was working, in Hegel's conception, was the state—not any state existing in his time but a constitutional organization guaranteeing freedom to all citizens. The journey of Spirit began in China, which had grasped the idea that one person (the emperor) was free; but freedom for only one person is in fact license for him and despotism for everyone else. Thus, the unfolding idea of freedom leads to the idea that, unless everyone is free, "freedom" will have no meaning. Yet freedom without limits is also self-contradictory (one person's freedom to swing his arms must be limited by the freedom of others not to be hit in the face). Thus, a structure of laws guarantees freedom rather than abridges it.

Hegel's philosophy of history was full of original and profound insights into the histories of China, India, Egypt, Greece, Rome, and the "Germanic world" (though it also included some dubious claims, especially about Africa). Although his most famous follower was Karl Marx, his influence was felt by many others as well. Many 19th-century historians who were not direct disciples of Hegel were nevertheless idealists of some sort; they focused on the cultures created by peoples and believed that the study of history used distinctive methods and was radically different from, but not inferior to, natural science.

JULES MICHELET

Jules Michelet is the archetypal Romantic historian. He had a conventionally successful academic career at the Collège de France until he was dismissed in 1851 for refusing to take an oath to Louis Napoleon, president of France and soon emperor of the French. "Academic," however, would be the least appropriate description of Michelet's histories. Michelet took an almost sensual pleasure in entering "catacombs of manuscripts, this wonderful necropolis of national monuments" whose contents were "not papers, but lives of men, of provinces, of people." What he did with the documents, however, was quite different. Distinguishing himself from two contemporaries, François Guizot and Augustin Thierry (he could have added the great German historian Leopold von Ranke), Michelet commented: "Guizot analyzes, Thierry narrates, I resurrect!"

In his effort to bring the past, in all its variety, back to life, Michelet did not hesitate to consult the people of his time: "I shut the books, and placed myself among the people to the best of my power; the lonely writer plunged again into the crowd, listened to their noise, noted their words." The people were France, the object of Michelet's passion. Through all the vicissitudes of its history, they remained its quasi-mystical essence; and Michelet exhorted them to retain their sense of national unity.

CHAPTER FOUR

THE NINETEENTH CENTURY TO THE PRESENT

U ntil the beginning of the 19th century, the history of historiography could be represented in a list of great and near-great individuals. Group efforts like those of the Bollandists or the Benedictines of St. Maur were the exception; almost all historians worked alone. History had no established place in most university curricula, being subsumed under rhetoric (or occasionally grammar) and studied mainly in faculties of law or theology. The universities, too, lacked intellectual vitality; Gibbon called the 14 months he spent at Oxford the most idle and unprofitable of his life. In Germany, where universities had always been more influential (almost all the great figures in German intellectual life had doctoral degrees), the characteristic institutional structure of contemporary historiography was being established.

JOHANN CHRISTOPH GATTERER AND THE GÖTTINGEN SCHOLARS

The centre of this activity was the university at Göttingen, in the electorate of Hannover. The electorate was ruled by the Hannoverian kings of England (George I through William IV), who, whether from tolerance or inattentiveness, allowed greater freedom of thought than did rulers in other parts of Germany. As a new university (founded 1737), Göttingen was less bound by traditional academic divisions, and it soon devoted itself especially to law and history rather than to philosophy or theology. Its rise to prominence began with the appointment in 1759 of Johann Christoph Gatterer (1727–99) to the chair of history. One of the first scholars to be interested in the history of historiography, Gatterer understood the institutional support that the new academic discipline would require. By 1763 the library of the university had grown to 200,000 volumes, making it one of the largest in Germany.

One of Gatterer's most important projects was a critical edition of sources for the study of German history, which ultimately came to fruition in the collection known as the *Monumenta Germaniae Historica* (*Historical Monuments of the Germans*). He also founded two historical journals (by 1791 there were 131 mainly historical journals in Germany) and a Historical Institute, an early type of seminar.

The scholars of Göttingen shared some of the philosophical interests of Enlightenment thinkers, including Montesquieu's empirical approach to law and politics. One of the Göttingen professors, for example, lectured on what he called *Statistik*, which at first was the study of mostly qualitative data about states but soon came to resemble modern statistics as numerical data became more widely available. What was most important about the Göttingen scholars was that they described states as they were rather than fantasizing about how they might have been.

LEOPOLD VON RANKE

Soon other German universities became centres of advanced historical research. This was particularly true of Berlin, which was the site of the Prussian Academy of Sciences (founded 1700) and the Humboldt University of Berlin (founded 1809–10), both of which attracted great scholars from all over the country.

The name that will always be associated with the latter institution, however, is that of Leopold von Ranke (1795–1886), who taught there

Oil portrait of von Ranke, painted by J. Schrader in 1868.
It is in the Nationalgalerie in Berlin, Germany.

for 37 years. His written works were only one avenue of his influence on 19th-century historiography. Ranke was an obscure Gymnasium (a state-run secondary school) teacher when, at the age of 29, he published *Geschichte der romanischen und germanischen Völker von 1494 bis 1514* (1824; *History of the Latin and Teutonic Nations from 1494 to 1514*). In the preface to the work he famously stated that, although history has been assigned the task of judging the past and giving lessons for the future, his work "will merely show how it actually was (*wie es eigentlich gewesen*)." The second volume, *Zur Kritik neuerer Geschichtsschreiber* (*Critique of Modern Historians*), established critical methods of historical scholarship that have since become normative. Ranke emphasized the acquisition of first-hand information and the tireless search for all relevant data, which he defined as "memoirs, diaries, letters, reports from embassies, and original narratives of eyewitnesses." He cited Guicciardini as an example of faulty historiographical practice, demonstrating that he invented the content of many reported speeches, that he could not have had any personal knowledge of many events about which he wrote, and that, even when he did have personal knowledge, he often copied from contemporary accounts.

Interestingly, Ranke's list of sources of relevant data omits what present-day historians would consider the most obvious and valuable source: state papers (the documents produced by public officials in performing official actions). Such documents were not generally available to historians when Ranke started to write, but, as a result of pressure from the growing historical profession, more and more archives were opened to them.

Shortly after Ranke's book was published, he was called to Berlin. He would have won no awards for lecturing, however. One of the many Americans drawn to the new temple of historical research described him as "a little round-faced man, with a baldish forehead, a high voice and thin hair." He "jerked out" his observations "like a garden fountain which keeps spurting up little futile jets and then stopping." But it was his seminars that established his influence.

Modeled on seminars in philology and Greek literature that Ranke had attended as a student, they offered a "laboratory" in historical method in which problems were posed, documents sought out and produced, and mutual criticism offered.

More than 100 historians passed through Ranke's seminar, including Heinrich von Sybel (1817–95) and Jacob Burckhardt (1818–97). Ranke's students established seminars of their own, and their hundreds of pupils were also disciples of Ranke. When Gabriel Monod (1844–1912), who would become one of the leading French historians of his generation, asked the great Hippolyte Taine (1828–92) whether he should go to Germany to study history, Taine answered yes. The Germans' superiority, he said, rested on two bases. They were philologists who went straight to original documents, but they were also philosophers, which gave them "the habit of generalizing and of seeing objects in masses."

Although Ranke has been regarded as a positivist who was concerned only with facts, the very intensity of his preoccupation with ascertaining those facts came from his conviction that history was, as he wrote, a "holy hieroglyph." He was as convinced as any medieval monk that history was the unfolding of a divine plan; for him, however, the plan required the existence of modern European nation-states. States, he wrote, were "thoughts of God"; by intuiting the idea or cultural principle incarnated in each nation, the historian could discern at least intimations of the divine plan. Accordingly, much of Ranke's own scholarship focused on the inner workings of the nation-states and their relationships with each other; for this his exploitation of the *relazioni*, or reports, of astute Venetian diplomats was especially important.

The conclusion of his life's work, however, was an unfinished universal history, published in nine volumes between 1881 and 1888. In an age of rampant nationalism, to which Ranke's histories had certainly contributed, his final legacy was a sort of cosmopolitanism.

NEW HISTORIES IN GERMANY

Although Ranke's influence was enhanced by his longevity (he lived to the age of 91), it was mainly due to the seductive synthesis he offered. He maintained that scholarship could produce historical truth; he held a conception of the divine will that linked it to the existing nation-states of 19th-century Europe; and he possessed a considerable literary gift. Even in Germany, however, his sway was never absolute, and by the end of the century his style of history was under assault from a number of directions.

Ranke's philosophy of history, which he usually articulated in prefaces or asides, was examined by Johann Gustav Droysen (1808–84) in a series of lectures eventually published as the *Historik*. Droysen maintained that Ranke's critical method and literary virtuosity had created an aura of scientific accuracy that shielded his faulty theistic interpretations. Rather than focusing on a core of ascertainable facts, however, Droysen emphasized how the same set of facts could be accounted for in different ways. The French Revolution, for example, could be the subject of at least four forms of discourse: investigative, narrative, didactic, and discussive (mixtures of these being found in most historical works). Of these, Droysen favoured the discussive because it was explicitly addressed to the relevance that historical knowledge might have to society. The past is inaccessible except through its "remains," which can be interpreted pragmatically, focusing on the aims of the actors in historical events; conditionally, stressing the material conditions under which actions take place; psychologically, comprising both character types and the element of individual personality and will; or ethically, contemplating the events under moral categories. By drawing attention to representative practices, by conceiving history as a discourse, and by arguing that no historian could give an unmediated account of "how it actually was," Droysen undercut the foundations on which Ranke's work rested, though this was all but unrecognized at the time.

Another attack came from those who believed that history should model itself after the natural sciences, especially physics. In their view, the reliance on intuition ensured that historiography would always be imprecise. Such critics also believed that the invocation of notions such as Spirit, Volk, or God was a mere mystification and that the focus on the individual or the particular rather than the general was misguided. Although very few historians fully embraced this position, some had ambitions in that direction. Among them was Karl Lamprecht (1856–1915), whose 12-volume *Deutsche Geschichte* (1891–1901; *German History*) elicited a furious response from historians in Germany. Lamprecht's transgressions were two-fold: he criticized the prevailing idealist approach to history, and he made social and cultural life, rather than the formation of the state, the central theme. His opponents accused him of having socialist sympathies (which was doubtful) and of attempting to undo the tradition of historiography that had made Germany admired throughout the world. Lamprecht sought to find laws of collective psychology governing the behaviour of Germans. His approach found few followers in Germany but had somewhat more influence in the United States. It was in any case a symptom of a widespread desire to find a different and more scientific basis for history.

NEW HISTORIES IN FRANCE

The most important voices calling for a new scientific history were heard in France and the United States. France had its own tradition of documentary criticism, stemming from the humanist scholars of the 16th century and stimulated by the founding of the École des Chartes (School of Paleography) in 1821. More resistant to German influence than any other European country, it also produced Auguste Comte (1798–1857), the prophet of scientific laws in history.

Auguste Comte, drawing by Tony Toullion, 19th century; in the Bibliothèque Nationale, Paris

AUGUSTE COMTE

The French philosopher who is known as the Father of Sociology is Auguste Comte (1798–1857). Comte advocated a science of society, which he named sociology. He urged the use of natural science techniques in the study of social life. He also originated positivism, a philosophic doctrine that incorporated his views on sociology.

Auguste Comte was born in Montpellier, France, on Jan. 19, 1798. His father, Louis, was a tax official. Auguste studied at the École Polytechnique, in Paris, from 1814 to 1816. In 1818 he became secretary to the Comte de St-Simon, a pioneer socialist. Beginning in 1826, Comte delivered private lectures to some of the leading French scholars and scientists of his day. These lectures became the basis of his most famous work, the six-volume *Course of Positive Philosophy* which was published between 1830 and 1842. In 1827, two years after his marriage to Caroline Massin, Comte suffered a mental breakdown. After his recovery he was on the staff of the École Polytechnique from 1832 to 1842. In his four-volume *System of Positive Polity* published between 1851 and 1854 Comte formulated a concept called "religion of humanity."

Comte is best known for his "law of the three stages." He died in Paris on Sept. 5, 1857.

Comte, inventor of the word "sociology" and often regarded as the father of the discipline, propounded an elaborate tripartite view of historical development. Humanity, he declared, had already passed through two stages, the theological and the philosophical. In the former, divinities or spiritual forces were believed to be the causes of natural and human events. In the philosophical period, natural laws were discovered, but the world of human events was still held to be indeterminate, and thought was confused by the belief in essences, teleologies, and other unobservable forces. The advent of the positive period was the French Revolution, which liberated humans from their theological fancies and philosophical mistakes. Henceforth, Comte prophesied, humans would rely only on what their senses told them and would seek out the laws that governed the human world. The aggregate of these laws would be sociology. Observations would be provided by historians; but historians, incapable of fully understanding their own discoveries, would rely on sociologists to place their observations under appropriate laws. This program, not surprisingly, did not appeal to historians, but it did offer an ideal for uniting all aspects of society in a single analytical framework.

In 1900 the French philosopher Henri Berr founded the social-science journal *Revue de Synthèse Historique*, which attracted contributions from some French historians. Berr's program for "historical synthesis" was more ambitious than any single historian could achieve; he called for teams of scholars from various disciplines to engage in empirical historical research with the aim of synthesizing their discoveries. Berr argued that no discipline could proceed without some sort of logical method that would involve hypothesis and synthesis as well as analysis. In this respect he agreed with the leading figure in French social science, Émile Durkheim (1858–1917), who established the journal *L'Année Sociologique* at about the same time. Although many French historians remained more traditional in their practice, Berr in 1907 recruited both Lucien Febvre (1878–1956) and Marc Bloch (1866–1944) as collaborators on the *Revue*. Together these men would challenge and revolutionize the study of history in France and in the rest of the world.

While at the University of Strasbourg, which then was on the margins of the French historical profession, Bloch and Febvre produced important works of their own, often focused on what became known as the history of *mentalités*, or popular attitudes and unconscious preconceptions. Although both eventually attained chairs at universities in

Paris, it was not until after World War II that they achieved a significant following—by then Bloch had been shot by the Nazis for his participation in the French resistance. After the war, the *Annales: Economies, Sociétés, Civilisations,* which they had founded in 1929 as *Annales d'histoire économique et sociale,* became the most influential historical journal in the world (the title was changed again in 1994, to *Annales: Histoire, Sciences Sociales*). Its impact was vastly enhanced by the capture by the Annalistes of the newly reconstituted Sixth Section of the École des Hautes Études (School of Higher Studies). Eventually, as a result of bureaucratic centralization in France and the willingness of the government to commit funds to higher education in order to gain cultural prestige, the directorate of the Sixth Section was virtually able to supervise historical research in the country.

NEW HISTORIES IN THE UNITED STATES

Whereas in 1875 there was hardly anything that could be called a historical profession in the United States, by 1900 the American Historical Association (AHA) and its journal, the *American Historical Review,* as well as a number of university Ph.D. programs in history, had been established. No clique of senior professors in the great universities could have achieved the sort of dominance in the United States that was possible in France or Germany, but there was nevertheless a struggle to create a group of historians, highly trained in the approved German manner, to claim the national history from the hands of the great amateurs such as Bancroft, Prescott, and Parkman. For a while amateurs coexisted amicably with the professionals (Bancroft was the second president of the AHA), but they soon withdrew to found more-congenial forums such as the *Mississippi Valley Historical Review* (now the *Journal of American History*). This prompted former U.S. president Theodore Roosevelt, who served as president of the AHA in 1912, to complain, not without reason, that the professionals were squeezing all the life out of history; their expertise was bought at the cost of pedantry in the profession and boredom among the public.

As they professionalized the teaching and writing of history, the new academic historians sought to dislodge the picture of the American past that had been painted by their predecessors. The first shock occurred in 1893, when Frederick Jackson Turner (1861–1932) delivered a paper on his "frontier thesis." Whereas Bancroft and most other leading historians of his generation had claimed that the early settlers of New England brought with them the germs of "Teutonic liberty," Turner—inspired by the announcement of the U.S. Census Bureau in 1890 that the western frontier was now "closed" (or entirely occupied)—declared that the decisive experience in American history had been that of pioneers as they pressed westward, settling the "empty" frontier. On the frontier, he declared, Americans developed their most distinctive characteristics: egalitarianism, self-help, and pragmatism.

Few important historical writings have ever rested on such a slender empirical basis. The "emptiness" of the frontier was an illusion created by the Census Bureau, which made no count of the Native Americans who inhabited these lands. Although the frontier thesis had been anticipated by Hegel, Turner's genius lay in bringing it forward at just the right time. The closing of the frontier did mark the end of a readily understandable period in American history.

Turner not only introduced a new conception of American history but also wrested the historical spotlight from Harvard and New England and shone it on his native Wisconsin and points west. His book *The United States, 1830–1850: The Nation and Its Sections* (1935), emphasized the importance of sectional conflict and demonstrated how cultural traits interacted with the natural environment; he thus achieved his goal of making history not just "the brilliant annals of the few" but also the story of "the degraded tillers of the soil, toiling that others might dream."

A generation of Turner's younger contemporaries, most notably Charles Beard (1874–1948), Carl Becker (1873–1945), and James Harvey Robinson (1863–1936), issued the first of many calls in the 20th century for a "new history." Although there was actually little novelty in the methods they advocated, they all aspired, like Turner, to reinterpret American history in the interest of a more democratic and rational society.

This desire to challenge conventional wisdom led to new works, including Beard's *An Economic Interpretation of the Constitution of the United States* (1913). Although he

Charles A. Beard (1874–1948)

did not claim that his was the only possible interpretation of the founding document, he asserted as a fundamental principle that

different degrees and kinds of property inevitably exist in modern society; party doctrines and "principles" originate in the sentiments and views which the possession of various kinds of property creates in the minds of the possessors; class and group divisions based on property lie at the basis of modern government; and politics and constitutional law are inevitably a reflex of these contending interests.

Beard neatly expressed his reinterpretation of the American Revolution by saying that it concerned the issue not just of home rule but of who should rule at home.

MARXIST HISTORIOGRAPHY

These historians, who were generally Progressives in politics, emphasized the importance of class conflict and the power of economic interests in their studies, revealing the influence of Karl Marx (1818–83). Marx and Friedrich Engels (1820–95) worked together in almost total isolation, and when Marx died it would have been difficult for a casual observer not to conclude that his ideas would disappear with him. By 1900, however, Marxism constituted the greatest challenge to the idealist tradition.

Despite the influence of philosophy, sociology, and economics, Marx's thought was profoundly historical. Hegel had taught him that history was constant change, produced by oppositions, reconciliations, and more oppositions. Acknowledging (in a way) this debt, Marx remarked that he found Hegel standing on his head and turned him right side up again. By this he meant that Hegel had mistaken the real motor of history: it was not the conflict of ideas but the conflict of social classes. Marx admitted, however, that this was not his own discovery; the "bourgeois" historians, such as Vico, had anticipated him. What Marx brought to the idea of class struggle was a conception of how it had developed and how it must eventually turn out.

Marx's understanding of class struggle was influenced by the work of the English economist David Ricardo (1772–1823), who had developed a model of how "perfect" markets work in a capitalist mode of production. Ricardo had made the conflicting interests of landlords, employers, and workers the centre of his picture of the economy. He argued that, because of Malthusian population dynamics, the wages of workers would always be held at or near subsistence levels. Marx extended the analysis by taking into account increases in population and in the productive powers of the economy. He correctly predicted—at a time when there were very few companies that employed more than 50 workers—that the size of capitalist enterprises would inexorably increase until giant corporations dominated the economy. Equally correctly, he predicted that the proportion of the labour force engaged in agriculture (over half in parts of Europe) and the number of small business owners would sharply decline, so that proletarians—those who had nothing to sell but their labour—would become the overwhelming majority of the population. Marx was less certain about the political consequences of these changes; by the end of his life he thought that capitalism might be brought to an end without violent revolution in some countries (the United States among them), and he saw that not all societies would pass through exactly the same sequence of changes. But he never lost his confidence that the system of private ownership of the means of production, in which enormous quantities of wealth accumulated in fewer and fewer hands, would inevitably be replaced by socialism.

None of this is history, properly speaking. The appeal of Marxism, for some historians, has been the rigour of this economic argument, which promises an eventual system based on moral precepts more appealing than "greed is good"; they also have been attracted to its suggestive implications for a unified approach to history. These are implications only, however. Marxist historiography, as a contemporary Marxist once said, is still "under construction." Marx's own historical writings are far from a mechanical application of his system. In his brilliant "Der 18te Brumaire des Louis Napoleon" (1852; "The Eighteenth Brumaire of Louis Bonaparte"), several classes, not just two, played important roles, and the political skill of Napoleon III is acknowledged—albeit grudgingly—as significant. Although some Marxist historians may still maintain a residual allegiance to the notion that ideas are a mere "super-structural" reflection of the material "base," the way this relationship is supposed to work has never been satisfactorily demonstrated, and this aspect of Marxism has largely been laid aside.

In recent times the idea has gained currency that Marxism has been "refuted by history." No successful revolution has broken out in any advanced capitalist country, and the collapse of the Soviet Union and the failure of the regimes in eastern Europe that called themselves Marxist has been taken as the conclusive demonstration that Marx was wrong. But "history" refutes nobody; only historians can do that, and other historians, looking at different evidence or reinterpreting the same, can in turn refute them. A more well-grounded objection might be that there is no way to refute Marx because his predictions are insufficiently precise; for example, he wrote that no mode of production gives way to its successor before it has exhausted all of its possibilities. The history of historiography suggests, however, that no grand scheme, whether of Augustine, Hegel, or Marx, can be "disconfirmed" by empirical evidence. They are different interpretations of history, more or less persuasive as one judges them on what are essentially aesthetic or moral grounds. The option to refuse to interpret in such a mode is of course always open.

CONTEMPORARY HISTORIOGRAPHY

The extraordinary expansion of higher education throughout the world in the first decades after World War II, and the prominent place that instruction in history occupied in colleges and universities, contributed to the dramatic growth in the historical profession in the second half of the 20th century. This in turn reflected a widespread public interest in—indeed, a fascination with—the past.

In the countries that fought in the war, especially the United States, returning veterans were given access to higher education. This created a mass market for teachers of history, again, especially in the United States, where it became common to inculcate in first-year students, under the rubric of "general education," courses in "Western civilization." (This was quickly and appropriately nicknamed "Plato to NATO"; its premise was that there was a continuous and relatively coherent Western tradition beginning in classical Greece and mutually enjoyed by the countries that happened to be members of the North Atlantic Treaty Organization.) With so many more people studying history, publishers in the English-speaking world began to produce cheap paperback editions even of historical monographs, making it possible for the first time to introduce undergraduates to real historical writing.

Borne on this tide were the graduate schools, which expanded their faculties and admitted Ph.D. candidates in numbers not seen before. Good doctoral dissertations (and even some bad ones) could attract the interest of publishers, and their authors usually had some choice of permanent employment. The buoyant publishing climate also encouraged historical journals to proliferate. None matched the impact of the *Annales*, but they often moved to the cutting edge of historical work. *Past and Present* was founded in 1952 at the University of Oxford with the provocative (but short-lived) subtitle "A Journal of Scientific History." Although committed to social history and drawing mainly on left-wing contributors, the journal never followed any rigid ideological line, and it quickly became the outstanding historical journal in English, rivaling the staid and traditional *English Historical Review* (founded 1885). Similar interests were addressed by *Comparative Studies in Society and History* (founded 1958) and the *Journal of Interdisciplinary History* (founded 1970), while *History and Theory* (founded 1960) became the first journal devoted to the theory of history.

CHAPTER FIVE

BRANCHES OF HISTORY, PART I: HISTORY OF THE ARTS, CULTURE, AND SOCIETY

Historiography does not consist solely of narrations of the major events of a given time period. It can also specifically address certain areas of human experience, particularly when they exert a large influence upon a time or a place. Historians now borrow from the work of other disciplines, particularly to construct an accurate larger picture of a culture or society. Many historians now include the history of the arts—such as dance, music, and visual arts—into their larger works, perhaps focusing on the audiences who were the consumers of arts in their culture or on how the arts expressed the unique spirit of the age. History is often now viewed not only through the perspectives of the major participants but also through the lives of ordinary people, the demographics of the time, and the interconnected experiences of women and families. Historians may also consider world history, including the question of whether there are so-called "master narratives" that explain the history of all cultures or peoples or places. Incorporating politics into history often means studying imperialism, including how the hegemony of an empire might affect the countries and peoples under its rule, even many years after they have gained freedom. All of these areas are both branches of history and components that can be added to more standard studies of history to make them richer and more accurate.

HISTORY OF ART

Histories have been written about architecture, sculpture, painting, music, dance, theatre, motion pictures, television, and literature. Despite essential differences, these forms of historiography have some common features. One is that they are almost invariably produced outside history departments and faculties. For this reason they have tended to be regarded as somewhat exotic specialties. Because the activities of artists are inevitably the central subject of most histories of the arts, such histories generally include formalistic analyses of artistic works. The distinction between history and philosophy in the case of art is thus less distinct than it is in other subject areas. Finally, performance traditions figure prominently in histories of music, dance, and theatre.

Historians are seldom satisfied with purely formal analyses of art and are seldom competent to make them. Historians have tried to integrate art history into their studies in three fundamental ways. The first is to consider the material conditions of production. Some of the issues are technical: what pigments were available to an artist? What special effects were possible in an Elizabethan theatre? Others relate to patronage, since most artists have always worked for commissions or pensions given to them by the rich (who in return got to appear in paintings, be mentioned in the prefaces of books, or attach their names to pieces of music). Finally, the working conditions and social status of artists have been investigated. Artists in past centuries had little social prestige; they were regarded as artisans and were organized in guild workshops with apprentices (or sons—Bach in Germany was almost a generic name for a musician).

A second approach, which became popular in the late 20th century, is to shift the emphasis from the artist to the audience. German literary critics carried this conception farthest in what they called *Rezeptionstheorie*. Applied to a work of literature, *Rezeptionstheorie* implies that the meaning of a work is determined not by the writer but by the reader, who is "implied" in the text. Sometimes scholars simply treat themselves as "the

71

Judith, oil on canvas by Giorgione, 1504; in the Hermitage Museum, St. Petersburg. 144 cm x 68 cm

reader," thus producing literary criticism rather than history. Occasionally, however, there is evidence of how ordinary readers reacted to novels (e.g., when readers wrote to magazines in which novels were serialized). The face-to-face nature of the performing arts makes it easier to determine how audiences responded to such works; there are famous stories of the disastrous premieres of Georges Bizet's opera *Carmen* or Giuseppe Verdi's *La traviata* and of the riot that erupted at the first performance of the ballet *Le Sacre du printemps (The Rite of Spring)*, by Igor Stravinsky and Serge Diaghilev. Reception theory has been particularly fruitful in the field of history of the moving image, since sophisticated means of measuring and evaluating audience responses are available (and, in television at least, slavishly followed).

The most ambitious—and most controversial—way of integrating art history into historiography relies on such notions as a zeitgeist, or spirit of an age. The originator of this approach was Jacob Burckhardt (1818–97), whose masterpiece, *The Civilization of the Renaissance in Italy*, begins with a chapter called "The State as a Work of Art" and argues that artistic production in the Renaissance is of a piece with politics and statecraft. Giambattista Vico's idea of the poetic tropes of an age of heroes, as contrasted with the prose of an age of irony, points in the same direction, as does G.W.F. Hegel's conception of Spirit coming to full self-consciousness through art, religion, and philosophy.

The history of painting has gained the most attention from scholars in part because paintings are traded commodities that often require authentication by experts. The authentication of modern paintings seldom requires the services of a professional historian, but works from previous centuries, especially those in which the cult of the individual artistic genius had not fully developed and paintings were not always signed, often do. One of the great art historians of the early 20th century, Bernard Berenson (1865–1959), borrowed a technique for attributions that depended on mannerisms of painting ears and noses, but he also overestimated his ability to identify paintings by the Italian Renaissance master Giorgione and others, incidentally making large sums for himself. In the late 20th century, art historians developed more-rigorous criteria for attribution, with the result that works once attributed to great artists such as Giorgione were demoted to "school of," "follower of," and the like. Art history is thus a field in which detecting forgeries is still a live issue. One of the great forgers of the 20th century, Hans van Meegeren, succeeded in passing off a number of his own canvases as works of the Dutch painter Johannes Vermeer.

Art historians have taken a variety of approaches. Such eminent figures as Ernst Gombrich (1909–2001) stoutly defended the establishment of a canon of indubitably great paintings, whereas Heinrich Wölfflin (1864–1945) treated "categories of beholding," which reveal the ways in which paintings create their effects. Paintings and works of sculpture also can have an intellectual content. One school of art historians, most prominently identified with Erwin Panofsky (1892–1968), studied iconology, or iconography, which consists of the formal analysis of visual motifs used to express thematic content or to identify important figures (thus, a skull or hourglass indicated death, and a figure carrying his skin over his shoulder referred to St. Bartholomew, who according to legend was flayed). To understand such paintings, knowledge of iconology is necessary but not sufficient. Iconologists have tried to move beyond providing simple lists of motifs to developing treatments of how motifs change and of what these changes indicate regarding the cultural and intellectual context of the painting.

Painting has not escaped the conceptual issue besetting most of the arts: how to identify an object as a work of art. Several developments challenge historians of contemporary art: the presentation of ordinary objects as "art"—such as the urinal that Marcel Duchamp submitted to a gallery as *The Fountain*; the rise of abstract painting; and portraits of soup cans by Andy Warhol. In *Transfiguration of the Commonplace* (1981), the American philosopher of art Arthur Danto argued that art is at an end, since there is now no way to distinguish between works of art and urinals and no distinct mode in which works of art can convey their intellectual content. Concurrently with this proclamation of the end of art came the question of whether art history has also come to an end. This is a typical postmodern provocation, of a piece with the claim that history as a whole has ended.

SOCIAL AND CULTURAL HISTORY

Many historians in the past echoed the calls of Jules Michelet or Thomas Carlyle to rescue ordinary people from the silence and condescension of history, but they generally lacked the means to go beyond anecdote, sentimentalism, and left-wing politics. Only since World War II (and here the journal *Annales: histoire, sciences sociales* was an extraordinary engine for progress) have historians developed the techniques to begin carrying out the program now called "history from the bottom up."

Historical demography, virtually created in the postwar period, was the armature around which much of modern social history was wound. Although the first theorist of population was the English economist Thomas Malthus, modern population studies developed mainly in France, the first country on the continent of Europe to experience declining population in the late 19th century. For the French, the main issue in population study was the cause of their population decline and how it might be reversed; for the English, the issue was why population had exploded from the mid-18th to the mid-19th century. Historical demography has many ramifications beyond the question of population size: migration, social mobility, household size and composition, and marriage patterns. The conventional wisdom in 1945 was that peasants in traditional European societies rarely moved from the parish of their birth; they lived in large multigenerational households and married young. Two generations of research proved that these views were either wholly false or true only of other parts of the world.

While some demographic historical techniques were developed by Louis Henry of the Institut National d'Études Démographiques (National Institute of Demographic Studies) in Paris, the Cambridge-based Group for the History of Population and Social Structure was responsible for helping to extend demographic studies to Japan, China, and most parts of Europe and North America. It served as a clearing-house for researchers on three continents and directed attention to types of evidence that were previously unknown. The picture of population that emerged from these researches was complex. A northwestern European pattern was visible in which until 1750 first marriages on average were late—mid-20s for women, late 20s for men. Households were small, and three-generation households were uncommon. One surprise was that the custom of kinfolk's living together was more common in industrialized than in agrarian areas. Another was the discovery that in England the main reason for the large population increase after 1750 was increased fertility, achieved through earlier marriages. On the other hand, south and west of a line from Trieste to St. Petersburg, people married much younger, and celibacy was rare. Households also tended to be larger, reaching remarkable sizes in the *zadrugas* (corporate family groups) of Yugoslavia and the Baltic provinces of the Russian Empire.

Such findings may seem only of specialized interest, but their ramifications are broad. Studies of family structure in colonial Massachusetts revealed that fathers were reluctant to agree to opening new lands for settlement, wishing to keep their sons within the household. Resentment of this by the sons may have played some role in the mind-set that led to the American Revolution. Migration too is a key to understanding not only the way that industrialization occurred (where did the new workers come from?) but also the settlement patterns of North America (the much higher propensity in the British than in the French or Spanish to leave their native parishes created an overwhelming British North American population). Migration is also a factor in social mobility; a 1964 study of Newburyport, Massachusetts, by Stephan Thernstrom ("Poverty and Progress: Social Mobility in a Nineteenth Century City") tested the reality of the American dream of rising to wealth. It was followed by others proclaiming a new urban history.

Quite different data helped create a history of sexuality. Extramarital or premarital sexual activity was indicated in figures on prenuptial or bridal pregnancy and birth of children to unmarried parents. Here again a surprise was that these seemed to be higher in 18th-century England—especially after 1750—than in France. Considering that in northwestern Europe people reached sexual maturity almost 10 years before they married, the relatively low level of illicit sexual activity suggests a general acquiescence to a repressive sexual morality. Although homosexual relations do not appear directly in these data, it may be significant that homosexual roles appear to have become available in the late 18th century just as the insistence on chastity began to weigh less heavily on heterosexuals. The history of sexuality was treated in depth by the French philosopher Michel Foucault in his final work, the multivolume *Histoire de la sexualité* (1976–84).

Foucault wrote important works in other areas of social history in which quantitative methods were relatively unimportant. Particularly significant was his treatment of "the great sequestration." In his *Surveillir et punir: naissance de la prison* (1975; *Discipline and Punish: The Birth of the Prison*), Foucault argued that prisons and hospitals (and by implication schools) developed as means of social control, and the oppressiveness of these institutions was only enhanced by high-minded rhetoric that declared them to be entirely devoted to their inmates' good. The image of the panopticon—a prison design by the English philosopher Jeremy Bentham that allowed for constant surveillance of the inmates—represented for Foucault the intimate link between power and knowledge and raised disturbing questions about who benefited from the activities of (for example) historians.

Protest and social control had long been a staple of social history. The former was the theme of the most-admired work of the period, *The Making of the English Working Class* (1963), by E.P. Thompson. Thompson defined the working class not as a statistical aggregate of people who had only their labour power to sell but as a group who between 1790 and 1840 came to consciousness of themselves as "working class." As the prospect of social revolution faded after 1968, however, historians, especially in the United States, began to investigate the absence of effective working-class protest in previous centuries. Although there was clear evidence of multiple acts of resistance by African American slaves, organized revolts were rare, especially after 1832. Eugene Genovese looked for an explanation in the work of the Italian Marxist philosopher Antonio Gramsci (1891–1937), who responded to the defeat of communist movements in Europe (except for Russia) after World War I by stressing the "hegemony" exercised by the ruling class through its control of education and other institutions that mold public opinion so that their rule appears natural and inevitable.

Historians are promiscuous borrowers from other disciplines, and in the late 20th century most borrowed techniques and concepts came

77

from anthropology—especially the symbolic anthropology espoused by Pierre Bourdieu and Clifford Geertz. Rather than seeking laws that govern social behaviour (the ambition of early sociology) or compiling quantitative data, symbolic anthropologists conceived human social relations as "texts" to be interpreted. The texts were exhibited as language, of course, but also as rituals of various sorts, and they had to be approached without any theoretical preconceptions. In *Deep Play: Notes on a Balinese Cockfight,* for example, Geertz claimed to "read" the event he witnessed. His method, which he called "thick description," was not far removed from traditional ethnography. It was also congenial, in its aversion to theory, to traditional historical practice, which was never comfortable with the attempt to explain historical events by subsuming them under laws.

Like much social history, cultural history could claim an ancestry from early works by Lucien Febvre (1878–1956) and Marc Bloch (1866–1944), who were early contributors to the social-science journal *Revue de Synthèse Historique.* In *Les Rois Thaumaturges: étude sur le caractère surnaturel attribué à la puissance royale, particulièrement en France et en Angleterre* (1924; *The Royal Touch: Sacred Monarchy and Scrofula in England and France*), Bloch investigated the belief that the kings of France and England possessed the quasi-magical power of curing scrofula (a disease affecting the bones and lymphatic glands) by touching sufferers; in *La Problème de l'incroyance au XVIe siècle: la religion de Rabelais* (1942; *The Problem of Unbelief in the Sixteenth Century: The Religion of Rabelais*), Febvre showed that the French writer and priest Francois Rabelais lived in a mental world in which atheism was not yet possible. These were studies of *mentalités*, which naturally often lay at the intersection between superstition and religion. Although the field was pioneered by French historians, Anglo-American scholars also studied *mentalités*; their works were concerned with the history of witchcraft and witch persecutions as well as with the decline in belief in magic.

Cultural history can be applied to nearly anything, and it has enriched understanding of a wide variety of phenomena. A good

MICROHISTORY

The 1980s were marked by the emergence of a different kind of cultural history, "microhistory," which consists essentially of a story about a person or persons. Two famous examples are Carlo Ginzburg's *The Cheese and the Worms* (1980), about the unorthodox cosmological and theological beliefs of a 16th-century Italian miller, and Natalie Zemon Davis's *The Return of Martin Guerre* (1983), a scholarly treatment of a famous true story about an imposter who took over the farm (and bed) of a substantial peasant in 16th-century France. Typically, microhistories featured central characters who were socially marginalized—exactly the sort likely to be overlooked by social history no less than by orthodox political history. Nevertheless, the marginal can be defined only relative to the typical, and the latter is something that only social history can provide.

illustration is the French Revolution, one of the most intensively studied events in European history. For at least a century after it took place it was treated as a political breakdown of the ancien régime, facilitated by the spread of the Enlightenment. Later, the economic and social organization of 18th-century France was studied—first by Marxists who saw it as a classic "bourgeois revolution" in which a feudal order was overthrown by a more progressive capitalist one and then by more-nuanced investigators who analyzed the various social and interest groups within the bourgeoisie and nobility. A cultural-historical approach emphasized the important role of cultural symbols—the Great Fear (prompted by rumours of an aristocratic conspiracy to overthrow the Third Estate), the Phrygian cap (an emblem of liberty during the revolution), the planting of "liberty trees," the great revolutionary festivals (such as the Festival of Federation, held in Paris in 1790 on the first anniversary of the storming

Youth wearing a Phrygian cap, marble, Roman copy of a Greek original, 4th century BCE; in the Fitzwilliam Museum, Cambridge, Eng.

of the Bastille)—and denied that they could be reduced to underlying inequalities and social tensions.

WOMEN'S HISTORY

In the 19th century, women's history would have been inconceivable because "history" was so closely identified with war, diplomacy, and high politics—from all of which women were virtually excluded. Although there had been notable queens and regents—such as Elizabeth I of England, Catherine de Medici of France, Catherine the Great of Russia, and Christina of Sweden—their gender was considered chiefly when it came to forming marriage alliances or bearing royal heirs. Inevitably, the ambition to write history "from the bottom up" and to bring into focus those marginalized by previous historiography inspired the creation of women's history.

One of the consequences of the professionalization of history in the 19th century was the exclusion of women from academic history writing. A career like that of Catherine Macaulay (1731–91), one of the more prominent historians of 18th-century England, was impossible one hundred years later, when historical writing had been essentially monopolized by all-male universities and research institutes. This exclusion began to break down in the late 19th century as women's colleges were founded in England (e.g., at the Universities of Oxford and Cambridge) and the United States. Some of these institutions, such as Bryn Mawr College in the U.S. state of Pennsylvania, had strong research agendas.

Although the earliest academic women's historians were drawn to writing about women, it cannot be said that they founded, or even that they were interested in founding, a specialty like "women's history." Alice Clark wrote *Working Life of Women in the Seventeenth Century* (1920), and Eileen Power wrote *Medieval English Nunneries c. 1275 to 1535* (1922), a definitive monograph, and *Medieval Women* (published posthumously in 1975). Many women (including some in the early

Rhoads Hall is a dormitory at Bryn Mawr College in Bryn Mawr, Pennsylvania.

history of the *Annales*) worked as unpaid research assistants and cowriters for their husbands, and it is doubtless that they were deprived of credit for being historians in their own right. An exception was Mary Ritter Beard (1876–1958), who coauthored a number of books with her more famous husband, Charles Beard, and also wrote *Women as a Force in History,* arguably the first general work in American women's history.

Since it was still possible in the 1950s to doubt that there was enough significant evidence on which to develop women's history, it is not surprising that some of the earliest work was what is called "contribution history." It focused, in other words, on the illustrious actions of women in occupations traditionally dominated by men. The other preoccupation

was the status of women at various times in the past. This was customarily evaluated in terms of comparative incomes, laws about ownership of property, and the degree of social freedom allowed within marriage or to unmarried women. In *The Creation of Patriarchy* (1986), Gerda Lerner, whose work chiefly concerned women in the United States, examined Mesopotamian society in an attempt to discover the ancient roots of the subjection of women. Explorations of the status of women also contributed to a rethinking of fundamental historical concepts, as in Joan Kelly's essay *Did Women Have a Renaissance?* (1977).

Another area of study, which was curiously slow to emerge, was the history of the family. Since in all times most women have been wives and mothers for most of their adult lives, this most nearly universal of female experiences would seem to dictate that women's historians would be especially interested in the history of the family. Yet for a long time few of them were. The history of the family was inspired primarily not by women's history but by advances made in historical demography, whose heavy quantification women's history generally avoided.

This partly explains why the majority of works in women's history have dealt with unmarried women—as workers for wages, nuns, lesbians, and those involved in passionate friendships. Evidence concerning the lives of these figures is in some ways easier to come by than evidence of maternal and family life, but it is also clear that feminist historians were averse to studying women as victims of matrimony—as they all too often were. There are, however, intersections between history of the family and women's history. A few historians have written works on family limitation (birth control) in the United States, for example; one of these scholars, Linda Gordon, raised the important question of why suffragists and other feminists did not as a rule support campaigns for family limitation.

Another way in which women's history can lead to a reassessment of history in general is by analyzing the concept of gender. Joan Scott has taken the lead in this effort. Gender, according to Scott and many others, is a socially constructed category for both men and women, whereas sex is a biological category denoting the presence or absence of certain chromosomes. Even physical differences between the sexes can be exaggerated (all fetuses start out female), but differences in gender are bound to be of greatest interest to historians. Of particular interest to women's historians are what might be called "gender systems," which can be engines of oppression for both men and women.

WORLD HISTORY

World history is the most recent historical specialty, yet one with roots in remote antiquity. The great world religions that originated in the Middle East—Judaism, Christianity, and Islam—insisted on the unity of humanity, a theme encapsulated in the story of Adam and Eve. Buddhism also presumed an ecumenical view of humankind. The universal histories that characterized medieval chronicles proposed a single story line for the human race, governed by divine providence; and these persisted, in far more sophisticated form, in the speculative philosophies of history of Vico and Hegel. Marxism too, although it saw no divine hand in history, nevertheless held out a teleological vision in which all humanity would eventually overcome the miseries arising from class conflict and leave the kingdom of necessity for the kingdom of plenty.

These philosophies have left their mark on world history, yet few historians (except for Marxists) now accept any of these master narratives. This fact, however, leads to a conceptual dilemma: if there is no single story in which all of humanity finds a part, how can there be any coherence in world history? What prevents it from simply being a congeries of national—or at the most regional—histories?

Modernization theorists have embraced one horn of this dilemma.

There is, after all, a single story, they argue; it is worldwide Westernization. Acknowledging the worth of non-Western cultures and the great non-European empires of the past, they nevertheless see the lure of Western consumer goods—and the power of multinational corporations—as irresistible. This triumphalist view of Western economic and political institutions drew great new strength from the downfall of the managed economies of eastern Europe and the emergence in China of blatant state capitalism. It is easier to claim worldwide success for capitalism than for democracy, since capitalism has been perfectly

Francis Fukuyama (1952–)

compatible with the existence of autocratic governments in Singapore, Taiwan, and Hong Kong; but history does suggest that eventually capitalist institutions will give rise to some species of democratic institutions, even though multinational corporations are among the most secretive and hierarchical institutions in Western society.

Modernization theory has been propounded much more enthusiastically by sociologists and political scientists than by historians. Its purest expression was *The Dynamics of Modernization* (1966), by Cyril Edwin Black, which made its case by studying social indexes of modernization, such as literacy or family limitation over time, in developing countries. Extending this argument in a somewhat Hegelian fashion, the American historian Francis Fukuyama provocatively suggested, in *The End of History and the Last Man* (1992), that history itself, as traditionally conceived, had ceased. This, of course, meant not that there would be no more events but that the major issues of state formation and economic organization had now been decisively settled in favour of capitalism and democracy. Fukuyama was by no means a simple-minded cheerleader for this denouement; life in a world composed of nothing but liberal nation-states would be, among other things, boring.

A much grimmer aspect of modernization was highlighted by Theodore H. Von Laue (1987) in *The World Revolution of Westernization*. Von Laue focused on the stresses imposed on the rest of the world by Westernization, which he saw as the root cause of communism, Nazism, dictatorships in developing countries, and terrorism. He declined to forecast whether these strains would continue indefinitely.

The stock objection to modernization theory is that it is Eurocentric. So it is, but this is hardly a refutation of it. That European states (including Russia) and the United States have been the dominant world powers since the 19th century is just as much a fact as that Europe was a somewhat insignificant peninsula of Asia in the 12th century. Some modernization theorists have caused offense by making it clear that they think European dominance is good for everybody, but it is noteworthy how many share the disillusioned view of the German sociologist Max Weber (1864–1920), who compared the rational bureaucracies that increasingly dominated European society to an "iron cage." More-valid criticisms point to the simplistic character of modernization theory and to the persistence and even rejuvenation of ostensibly "premodern" features of society—notably religious fundamentalism.

A considerably more complex scheme of analysis, world-systems theory, was developed by Immanuel Wallerstein in *The Modern World System* (1974). Whereas modernization theory holds that economic development will eventually percolate throughout the world, Wallerstein believed that the most economically active areas largely enriched themselves at the expense of their peripheries. This was an adaptation of Vladimir Ilyich

Lenin's idea that the struggle between classes in capitalist Europe had been to some degree displaced into the international economy, so that Russia and China filled the role of proletarian countries. Wallerstein's work was centred on the period when European capitalism first extended itself to Africa and the Americas, but he emphasized that world-systems theory could be applied to earlier systems that Europeans did not dominate. In fact, the economist André Gunder Frank argued for an ancient world-system and therefore an early tension between core and periphery. He also pioneered the application of world-systems theory to the 20th century, holding that "underdevelopment" was not merely a form of lagging behind but resulted from the exploitative economic power of industrialized countries. This "development of underdevelopment," or "dependency theory," supplied a plot for world history, but it was one without a happy ending for the majority of humanity. Like modernization theory, world-systems theory has been criticized as Eurocentric. More seriously, the evidence for it has been questioned by many economists, and while it has been fertile in suggesting questions, its answers have been controversial.

A true world history requires that there be connections between different areas of the world, and trade relations constitute one such connection. Historians and sociologists have revealed the early importance of African trade (Columbus visited the west coast of Africa before his voyages to the Americas, and he already saw the possibilities of the slave trade), and they have also illuminated the 13th-century trading system centring on the Indian Ocean, to which Europe was peripheral.

Humans encounter people from far away more often in commercial relationships than in any other, but they exchange more than goods. William H. McNeill, the most eminent world historian, saw these exchanges as the central motif of world history. Technological information is usually coveted by the less adept, and it can often be stolen when it is not offered. Religious ideas can also be objects of exchange. In later work, McNeill investigated the communication of infectious diseases as an important part of the story of the human species. In this he contributed to an increasingly lively field of historical studies that might loosely be called ecological history.

ECOLOGICAL HISTORY

Focusing on the biological substrate of history can sometimes capture a vital element of common humanity. This was an early topic for the *Annales* historians, who were often trained in geography. Emmanuel Le Roy Ladurie grounded his great history of the peasants of Languedoc in the soil and climate of that part of France, showing how the human population of the ancien régime was limited by the carrying capacity of the land. He went on to write a history of the climate since the year 1000. Even more influential were the magisterial works of Fernand Braudel (1902–85), perhaps the greatest historian of the 20th century. Braudel's *La Méditerranée et le monde méditerranéen à l'époque de Philippe II* (1949; *The Mediterranean and the Mediterranean World in the Age of Philip II*) had a political component, but it seemed almost an afterthought. Although it was not a world history, its comprehensive treatment of an entire region comprising Muslim and Christian realms and the fringes of three continents succeeded in showing how they shared a similar environment. The environment assumed an even greater role in Braudel's *Civilisation matérielle et capitalisme, XVe–XVIIIe siècle* (vol. 1, 1967; vol. 2–3, 1979; *Civilization and Capitalism, 15th–18th Century*). Although some of its claims seemed designed to shock conventional historical sensibilities—the introduction of forks into Europe, he wrote, was more important than the Reformation—no historical work has done more to explore the entire material base on which civilizations arise

One of the most important links between ecological history and world history is the so-called Columbian exchange, through which pathogens from the Americas entered Europe and those from Europe devastated the indigenous populations of the Americas. The Native Americans got much the worse of this exchange; the population of Mexico suffered catastrophic losses, and that of some Caribbean islands was totally destroyed. The effect on Europeans was much less severe. It is now thought that syphilis entered Europe from Asia, not the Americas.

Overt moralizing in historiography tends to attract professional criticism, and historians in Europe and the United States, where nation-states have long been established, no longer feel the moral obligation that their 19th-century predecessors did to exalt nationalism. They can therefore respond to global concerns, such as the clear-cutting of rainforests and global warming. It has become obvious that the world is a single ecosystem, and this may require and eventually evoke a corresponding world history.

SUBALTERN HISTORY

There is, however, a powerful countertendency: subaltern history. "Subaltern" is a word used by the British army to denote a subordinate officer, and "subaltern studies" was coined by Indian scholars to describe a variety of approaches to the situation of South Asia, in particular in the colonial and postcolonial era. A common feature of these approaches is the claim that, though colonialism ended with the granting of independence to the former colonies of Britain, France, the United States, and other empires, imperialism did not. Instead, the imperial powers continued to exert so much cultural and economic hegemony that the independence of the former colonies was more notional than real. Insisting on free trade (unlimited access to the domestic markets of the former colonies) and anticommunism (usually enforced by autocratic governments), the old empires, as the subaltern theorists saw it, had reverted to the sort of indirect rule that the British had exerted over Argentina and other countries in the 19th century.

The other belief that united subaltern theorists is that this hegemony should be challenged. *Orientalism* (1978), by the literary critic Edward Said, announced many of the themes of subaltern studies. The Orient that Said discussed was basically the Middle East, and the Orientalism was the body of fact, opinion, and prejudice accumulated by western

European scholars in their encounter with it. Said stressed the enormous appetite for this lore, which influenced painting, literature, and anthropology no less than history. It was, of course, heavily coloured by racism, but perhaps the most insidious aspect of it, in Said's view, was that Western categories not only informed the production of knowledge but also were accepted by the colonized countries (or those nominally independent but culturally subordinate). The importation of Rankean historiography into Japan and Russia is an example. The result has been described rather luridly as epistemological rape, in that the whole cultural stock of colonized peoples came to be discredited.

Although originally and most thoroughly applied to the Middle East and South Asia, subaltern history is capable of extension to any subordinated population, and it has been influential in histories of women and

Edward Said (1935–2003)

of African Americans. Its main challenge to world history is that most subaltern theorists deny the possibility of any single master narrative that could form a plot for world history. This entails at least a partial break with Marxism, which is exactly such a narrative. Instead, most see a postmodern developing world with a congeries of national or tribal histories, without closures or conventional narratives, whose unity, if it has one at all, was imposed by the imperialist power.

The project of bringing the experience of subordinated people into history has been common in postwar historiography, often in the form of emphasizing their contributions to activities usually associated with elites. Such an effort does not challenge—indeed relies on—ordinary categories of historical understanding and the valuation placed on these activities by society. This has seemed to some subaltern theorists to implicate the historian in the very oppressive system that ought to be combated. The most extreme partisans of this combative stance claim that, to resist the hegemonic powers, the way that history is done has to be changed. Some feminists, for example, complain that the dominant system of logic was invented by men and violates the categories of thought most congenial to women. This is one of the reasons for the currency and success of postmodernist and postcolonialist thought. It licenses accounts of the past that call themselves histories but that may deviate wildly from conventional historical practice.

Such histories have been particularly associated with a "nativist" school of subaltern studies that rejects as "Western" the knowledge accumulated under the auspices of imperialism. An instructive example was the effort by Afrocentric historians to emphasize the possible Egyptian and Phoenician origins of classical Greek thought. Martin Bernal, for example, tried to show in *Black Athena* (1987) that the racist and anti-Semitic Orientalist discourse of the late 19th century (particularly but not exclusively in Germany) obscured the borrowings of the classical Greeks from their Semitic and African neighbours. That there were borrowings, and that Orientalist discourse was racist and anti-Semitic, is beyond doubt, but these are findings made through ordinary historical investigation—whose conventions Bernal did not violate, despite the speculative character of some of his conclusions. How much distortion there was would also seem to be an ordinary, though difficult, historical question (made more difficult by the claim that the Egyptians had an esoteric and unwritten philosophical tradition that has left no documentary traces but that may have been imparted to Greek thinkers). But no historian could accept the claim that Aristotle gained knowledge from the library at Alexandria, since it was not built until after his death. If the idea that effects cannot precede causes is merely a culture-bound presupposition of Western-trained historians, then there is no logical basis for rejecting even a claim such as this. The nativist subaltern historians deserve credit at least for raising this issue (though, of course, not with such extreme examples). However, the price to be paid is high: if there are no logical categories that are not culture-bound, then people from different cultures cannot have a meaningful argument—or agreement—because these require at least some mutual acceptance of what will count as evidence and how reasoning is to be done. Most subaltern historians have therefore steered between the Scylla of contribution history and the Charybdis of nativism, and their emphasis on studying the mass of the people rather than colonial elites has had a powerful effect not only on the history of Asia and Africa but also on that of Europe and even the United States.

CHAPTER SIX

BRANCHES OF HISTORY, PART II: BIOGRAPHY, PSYCHOHISTORY, AND INTELLECTUAL HISTORY

There are additional branches of history, which make use of other sciences and approaches to study the events and people of a specific era. Biography, or biographical history, approaches history through the lives of prominent individuals. Biographers may also attempt to explain their subjects' behavior by applying psychological theories, an approach that is the basis of a branch of history known as psychohistory. Finally, intellectual history explores the propagation and dissemination of ideas; it also considers the relatively unarticulated feelings of ordinary people, including even popular delusions.

BIOGRAPHY AND PSYCHOHISTORY

Ancient biography, especially the entire genre of hagiography, subordinated any treatment of individual character to the profuse repetition of edifying examples. They were generally about eminent men, but women could qualify as subjects by being martyred. Although biographies written in the Italian Renaissance, such as that of Giorgio Vasari, began to resemble modern biographies, those written in the Northern Renaissance were still of great public figures, by someone who knew them. They were almost totally lacking in psychological insight, personality being swathed in thick layers of virtue. For example, the life of Thomas More, written by his son-in-law, does not even mention that More was the author of *Utopia* (1516). In the 17th century, however, Izaak Walton (better known today for his classic treatise on angling) wrote some lives of literary figures, adding heroes of culture to those of war and politics as appropriate subjects. The renowned Samuel Johnson (1709–84) has the distinction of being both a biographer (of English poets) and the subject of the biography by James Boswell, *Life of Johnson* (1791), which was roughly as important for biography as Edward Gibbon's *Decline and Fall of the Roman Empire* (1776–88) was for historiography.

Biographers of contemporaries are often faced with one of two unique challenges. They sometimes discover that the letters, diaries, and other personal documents of the subject that are most necessary for writing the biography have been destroyed, sometimes precisely to prevent a biography from being written. Writers of authorized biographies, however, are often granted privileged access to these materials but are somewhat constrained by the commission. Even when the biographer is not dependent on the subject (or literary executor) for the necessary sources, the relationship between the two persons can be intense. There is likely to be some—perhaps overriding—emotional attraction on the part of the biographer to the person he wishes to write about. Some writers believe that the biographer must become intimately acquainted with the mind and emotions of the subject. This requirement is obviously easier to meet if the two are close friends, but biographers can also generate deep empathy with people long dead. However, it seems to be fascination, not admiration, that is essential, since good biographies have been written by authors who came to despise their subjects. Otherwise there presumably could never have been good biographies of Adolf Hitler or Joseph Stalin.

Writing the life of a major writer or artist presents different problems—and opportunities—from those presented in writing the life of a statesman. It also makes a vast difference whether or not one is writing about a contemporary. Biographers face the problem of access to private collections as well as the problem of the quality of those collections, which vary enormously in size and informativeness. For example, whereas only about 300 often terse letters by the American novelist Herman Melville survive, there are about 15,000 extant letters by the American writer Henry James—this after James had burned all his copies of his letters and everything else that might have been useful to a biographer.

Although at times faced with the willful destruction of the personal papers of their subjects, almost every biographer of a contemporary figure faces an embarrassment of documents and must at times envy the biographer of such sparsely documented figures as William Shakespeare. Victorian biographers generally surrendered to a plethora of sources by writing extremely long accounts of the life and times of statesmen, larded with extensive verbatim quotations from their correspondence and speeches. The English critic Lytton Strachey (1880–1932) ridiculed these multivolume monuments piled on the bones of the dead, and in his *Eminent Victorians* (1918) he completely changed the course of biography as a literary genre. In four short and witty sketches of Florence Nightingale, Henry Cardinal Manning, Gen. Charles George Gordon, and Thomas Arnold, Strachey gave vent to all that a modernist generation that had survived World War I felt for its pious and overbearing predecessors. Strachey was particularly adept at pouncing upon and pointing out instances of unconscious hypocrisy. Although his brother James Strachey was the first translator of Sigmund Freud in England, it is not clear that Lytton Strachey had read anything by him, but Freud's ideas were in the air and could not fail to interest a biographer imbued with "the hermeneutics of suspicion."

Those seeking a balanced account of these four great Victorians will not find it in Strachey's pages. Yet though he was sometimes unfair and

LYTTON STRACHEY

Lytton Strachey (1880—1932) was an English biographer and critic who opened a new era of biographical writing at the close of World War I. Adopting an irreverent attitude to the past and especially to the monumental life-and-letters volumes of Victorian biography, Strachey proposed to write lives with "a brevity which excludes everything that is redundant and nothing that is significant." He is best known for *Eminent Victorians*—short sketches of the Victorian idols Cardinal Manning, Florence Nightingale, Thomas Arnold, and Gen. Charles "Chinese" Gordon.

After studying at Cambridge (1899–1903), Strachey lived in London, where he became a leader in the artistic, intellectual, and literary Bloomsbury group (q.v.). He published critical writings, especially on French literature, but his greatest achievement was in biography. After *Eminent Victorians* (1918) and *Queen Victoria* (1921), he wrote *Elizabeth and Essex* (1928) and *Portraits in Miniature* (1931). Treating his subjects from a highly idiosyncratic point of view, he was fascinated by personality and motive and delighted in pricking the pretensions of the great and reducing them to somewhat less than life-size. His aim was to paint a portrait; and though this led to caricature and sometimes, through tendentious selection of material, to inaccuracy, he taught biographers a sense of form and of background, and he sharpened their critical acumen.

His defects as a biographer arose mainly from his limited vision of life. He saw politics largely as intrigue, religion as a ludicrous anachronism, and personal relations as life's supremely important facet. Though bitterly attacked during his lifetime and after, Strachey remains a phenomenon in English letters and a preeminent humorist and wit.

Lytton Strachey, c. 1920

Mona Lisa, oil painting on a poplar wood panel by Leonardo da Vinci, c. 1503–06

sacrificed judiciousness to witticisms, Strachey became a model for future biographers who wanted to escape from the thousand-page tomes that monumentalized great statesmen and authors. This meant touching subjects that had previously been passed over, either through prudery or respect for privacy. Thus, the poet Robert Southey's life of Horatio Nelson, the English naval hero, denied that there was any "crudity" (sexual intercourse) in his relationship with Lady Hamilton. As late as 1951 Roy Harrod published a biography of the influential economist John Maynard Keynes that did not mention homosexuality. By contrast, many biographers in the later 20th century considered their primary task to be the interpretation of their subject's psychosexual development.

For this enterprise there are, of course, psychological theories. Unfortunately, there are all too many of them. Even if the biographer decides on depth psychology—and there are alternatives—the choice is not much simplified. Although Freudian psychoanalysis has pretty much swept the field in the United States, there are still European scholars influenced by Carl Jung. Furthermore, there are a bewildering variety of alternative Freudian theories—not a few of them propounded by the master himself. So it is not altogether clear what orthodox Freudianism is, but it would emphasize the importance of instinctual drives and of experiences in early childhood.

Even for the psychoanalyst, these are the most difficult areas, and the most difficult time, of human life to get evidence about; this is why full analyses run toward the interminable. For the biographer with little or no access to reports of the dreams of his subject—very few of anyone's dreams have been recorded—or to the other ways in which the unconscious most often gives itself away, "psychobiography" inevitably becomes speculative. Freud's own ventures into the field are not reassuring. Art historians have pointed out that the smile of the Mona Lisa was a standard way of painting a certain emotion, not necessarily an unconscious revival of a childhood sexual memory of Leonardo da Vinci. American political historians have been even more dismissive of the joint effort by Freud and William C. Bullitt to write a psychological biography of Woodrow Wilson.

In practice, many psychohistorians have adopted the psychoanalytic theories of the analyst who analyzed them (a few have become psychoanalysts themselves). The problem of getting evidence for psychobiographies is easier, however, if one accepts the American revision of Freudianism known as ego psychology. This theory denies that personality is fixed after the age of five; it can still be substantially influenced by what goes on later, especially in adolescence. The most influential exponent of this approach for biographers was Erik Erikson, who propounded an eight-stage theory of the normative life course and wrote substantial psychobiographies of Martin Luther and Mahatma Gandhi. The overriding theme of both was the way in which an individual leader, working out his own "identity crisis," was also able to do what Erikson called "the dirty work of his society." This reinterpretation of the "great man" theory of history (which holds that the course of history is determined by a few individuals) made it possible to argue not only that culture influences adolescent personality development but also that adolescent personality development might at times powerfully influence culture.

Construal of evidence by psychobiographers can be radically different from normal historical practice (as reviewers were not slow to remind Erikson). Historians are accustomed to "weighing" the evidence, almost in a literal sense. Frequent iteration of an attitude generally persuades, even if there are one or two exceptions. For the psychobiographer, an apparently trivial event or slip of the pen can be the vital clue to the personality of the subject. Luther's toilet habits, treatment of Hitler's mother by a Jewish doctor who used a gas therapy in an attempt to cure her cancer, or Baudouin I of Belgium's auto accident a few years before World War II would be dismissed by many historians as of dubious relevance to public careers; to psychobiographers they can be the foundation of an entire work.

Although they cannot study dreams, biographers have in the writings of poets and novelists a kind of public dream. Deciphering these for their disguised biographical content runs against current literary critical as well as historiographical orthodoxy, yet many biographers of writers place great stock in their ability to do this. The conventional historian, asked to describe Nathaniel Hawthorne's state of mind during the years he lived at Salem, would look for the various documents he produced while he was there. But these throw little light on the question. The literary biographer, in contrast, claims to be able to answer it by interpreting the works that Hawthorne wrote while he was there. One has even said that, no matter how much other, more usual evidence might turn up, he would still stay with what he drew from his interpretation.

Like cliometrics, psychohistory was a fashionable methodology in the 1960s and '70s but has become distinctly less fashionable since. It has to a degree been discredited by the excesses of some of its partisans, and its difficulties proved greater than most of its early advocates had expected. Just as biography has made a contribution to historiography generally through prosopography (the study of related persons within a given historical context), collective psychology has reappeared in a psychoanalytic study of early adherents of Nazism and in the history of *mentalités* (semiarticulated or even unconsciously held beliefs and attitudes that set limits to what is thinkable. Freud's exercise in group dynamics, *Massenpsychologie und Ich-analyse* (1921; *Group Psychology and the Analysis of the Ego*), was appropriated by Henry Abelove for his fine study *The Evangelist of Desire: John Wesley and the Methodists* (1990). These are signs that neither the biographical nor the psychohistorical impulse has exhausted its energy.

INTELLECTUAL HISTORY

"All history," as R.G. Collingwood said, "is the history of thought." One traditional view of history, now discarded, is that it is virtually synonymous with the history of ideas—history is composed of human actions; human actions have to be explained by intentions; and intentions cannot be formed without ideas. On a grander scale, the doctrines of Christianity were the core of the providential universal histories that persisted until the 18th century, since the acceptance—or rejection—of Christian ideas was considered history's master plot. When the providential argument in its simpler medieval form lost credibility, it was reformulated by Vico, with his conception of the tropes appropriate to the different ages of humanity, and by Hegel, whose "objective" idealism identified the development of Spirit, or the Idea, as the motor of history. In the techniques of historical investigation too, the history of ideas was the source for the hermeneutical skills required for reading complex tests. The interpretation of ancient laws and religious doctrines was the workshop in which were forged the tools that were subsequently used in all historical work.

It was not until the speculative schemes that identified the development of ideas with the historical process were generally discredited, and its hermeneutic techniques thoroughly naturalized elsewhere, that intellectual history became a specialty—the first specialized field to supplement the traditional historical specialties of political, diplomatic, and military history. It emerged slightly earlier than social history, and for a time the two were allies in a joint struggle to gain acceptance. The incompatibility—indeed, antagonism—between the two emerged only later.

Confusion can arise because history of ideas and intellectual history are sometimes treated as synonyms. The former is properly the name of a field of study in which ideas themselves are the central subject. The most sophisticated approach to the history of ideas was formulated by Arthur Lovejoy (1873–1962). Lovejoy focused on what he called "unit ideas," such as the notion of a Great Chain of Being extending from God through the angels to humans down to the least-complicated life-forms. Lovejoy traced this idea from its classical roots through the 19th century in both philosophical and literary elaborations. Philosophical or theological doctrines (e.g., Plato's theory of Forms, or Manichaeism, a dualist religious movement founded in Persia) lend themselves best to the unit-idea mode of study. One difficulty with the history of unit ideas, however, is that it is often difficult to establish the identity of an idea through time. The term *natural law*, for example, meant quite different things to Stoic philosophers, to Thomas Hobbes, to John Locke, and to the prosecutors of Nazi war criminals at the Nürnberg trials (1945–46); the meaning of the same words can change radically. This drives the historian to the Oxford English Dictionary or its equivalents for other languages to get a first take on the history of meaning changes. This step, however, must be supplemented by extensive reading in the contemporary literature, not only to see what semiotic load the words bear but also to see what controversies or contrary positions might have been in the mind of the writer.

The phrase *intellectual history* did not come into common usage until after World War II. It seems to owe its first currency to *The New England Mind: From Colony to Province* (1953), by Perry Miller (1905–63), who required it for his approach to the complex of religious, political, and social ideas and attitudes in Massachusetts in the 17th and 18th centuries. The focus of intellectual history has been not on the formal analysis of ideas, as in the history of ideas, but on the conditions of their propagation and dissemination. It also considers not just the formally articulated

Jacques Derrida in 2001

ideas of theorists or poets but also the sentiments of ordinary people. Even popular delusions come within the ambit of intellectual history; in this respect it intersects studies within psychohistory and the cultural history of *mentalités*.

Perhaps because their area of study is so ill-defined, intellectual historians have been unusually reflective and argumentative about the methods appropriate to their work. One methodological controversy was initiated in the 1960s by Quentin Skinner. Skinner questioned the custom in political philosophy of identifying certain "eternal" questions (such as "Why does anyone have an obligation to obey the state?") and then arraying various political texts according to the answers they give. This procedure, he argued, led to invalid historical conclusions, since the eternal questions were the constructions of modern political philosophers and reflected modern concerns. Taking his cue from the ordinary language philosophy of John Langshaw Austin and other postwar Oxford philosophers, Skinner contended that the task for the historian of political thought was to discover what effect the writer of a text intended it to have.

Skinner's best example was *Locke's Second Treatise of Civil Government* (1690), which for generations had been paired with Thomas Hobbes's Leviathan as one of two versions of a social contract theory. Skinner and his colleague John Dunn started from the obvious but often ignored fact that there was a first treatise by Locke that refuted the idea that political power devolved from the power that God gave to Adam. Absurd as this idea seems to contemporary philosophers, it nevertheless commanded widespread assent in 17th-century Britain. Similarly, a great deal of controversial writing was then done by clergymen, and Locke (as is evident from his many quotations of the Anglican divine Richard Hooker) participated actively in this discourse. On the other hand, there is very little evidence that Locke was responding to Hobbes.

In no branch of history has the challenge of postmodernism and deconstruction been felt more keenly than in the history of ideas. Here the goal has been to interpret past texts; the intentions of the author, as revealed in those texts, set limits to possible interpretations even where they do not mandate a single one. Deconstructionists such as Jacques Derrida assert that the intentions of the author can never be known and would be irrelevant even if they could be. All that an interpreter has is the text—thus, Michel Foucault, drawing upon the work of literary critic Roland Barthes, declared the "death" of the author. No single meaning can be assigned to the text, because what it does not say may be more significant than what it does. Even what it does say cannot be reduced to a stable meaning, because of the intrinsic opacity and slipperiness of language. (Most words in ordinary usage have several different definitions; there is no way to use them so as to totally exclude all traces of the other meanings. Puns, of which Derrida was fond, illustrate these "surplus" meanings.)

The subversiveness of such views for the traditional practice of the history of ideas is obvious. Derrida's advocates presented his ideas as liberating and as allowing critics to exercise the same creativity as imaginative writers. The apparent concession to total relativism, however, has seemed too high, not least because it renders the deconstructionist position vulnerable to the paradox of relativism (if the deconstructionist is right that there are no stable meanings, then there is no stable meaning to the assertion that there are no stable meanings, in which case the deconstructionist position cannot even be formulated). Derrida occasionally complained of being misread. But the deconstructionist position is not absurd, nor can it be refuted by saying that few historians have accepted it.

CHAPTER SEVEN

BRANCHES OF HISTORY, PART III: DIPLOMATIC, ECONOMIC, MILITARY, AND POLITICAL HISTORY

Istory has always focused heavily on political, economic, and military developments. Ancient Greek and Roman historians considered military exploits and wars to be the primary reason to chronicle historical events. It is still a vital part of the historical record, although the approach to studying war has shifted from studying tactics and battles and military leaders to exploring the personal experiences of those who fought. In the same way, while politics has always occupied a central role in traditional histories, there has been an attempt by newer political historians to view this branch of history in a more scientific manner. For example, they use statistics and demographics to trace relationships between people, their voting habits, and the officials they elect. Diplomatic history is obviously related to both military and political history. One of the questions it considers is how a country's political and national ideologies affect its diplomatic relationships with other political entities. Contemporary diplomatic history can be a difficult area of study, because national-security concerns often making access to documents and government officials complicated or even impossible. Like political history, economic history also makes use of specialized tools, including the use of statistics and the application of economic theory to historical situations or institutions.

All of these branches of history add even more lenses through which to view history, ancient or recent, and contribute to a richer understanding of a particular event or time.

DIPLOMATIC HISTORY

Diplomatic history comes closer than any other branch of history to being "completed"—not in the sense that everything about past diplomatic relationships has been discovered but rather in the sense that apparently all the techniques proper to it have been perfected. Unfortunately, the sharpest set of tools is useless without the matter on which to work, and in this respect historians of 20th- and 21st-century diplomacy are at a considerable disadvantage compared with those of earlier periods.

There is probably no branch of history—excepting perhaps biography—in which access to sources is so tricky, or their interpretation so difficult. The main obstacle to contemporary diplomatic history is the shroud of security that almost every state has thrown over its records, especially states that have mixed conventional diplomacy with covert operations. Historians typically have to wait 30 years or more for state papers to be declassified. The photocopying machine, however, created new opportunities for diplomatic leaks, most notably the publication in 1971 of the Pentagon Papers, which revealed American planning for military intervention in Indochina from World War II until 1968.

After coming to power in the Russian Revolution of 1917, the Bolsheviks gave historians of the origins of World War I a bonanza by publishing the secret dispatches of the tsarist government, which for the first time revealed the web of alliances and secret agreements that had allowed a Balkan incident eventually to embroil all the great powers. Each government thereupon published its own editions of documents. This plethora of documentation did not allow historians to reach consensus about the responsibility for starting the war, but the blame was certainly allocated more evenly than it had been in the "war guilt" clause of the Treaty of Versailles. Many historians in Britain and the United

THE PENTAGON PAPERS

The Pentagon Papers contain a history of the U.S. role in Indochina from World War II until May 1968 and were commissioned in 1967 by U.S. Secretary of Defense Robert S. McNamara. They were turned over (without authorization) to the *New York Times* by Daniel Ellsberg, a senior research associate at the Massachusetts Institute of Technology's Center for International Studies.

The 47-volume history, consisting of approximately 3,000 pages of narrative and 4,000 pages of appended documents, took 18 months to complete. Ellsberg, who worked on the project, had been an ardent early supporter of the U.S. role in Indochina but, by the project's end, had become seriously opposed to U.S. involvement. He felt compelled to reveal the nature of U.S. participation and leaked major portions of the papers to the press.

On June 13, 1971, the *New York Times* began publishing a series of articles based on the study, which was classified as "top secret" by the federal government. After the third daily installment appeared in the *Times*, the U.S. Department of Justice obtained in U.S. District Court a temporary restraining order against further publication of the classified material, contending that further public dissemination of the material would cause "immediate and irreparable harm" to U.S. national defense interests.

The *Times*—joined by the *Washington Post*, which also was in possession of the documents—fought the order through the courts for the next 15 days, during which time publication of the series was suspended. On June 30, 1971, in what is regarded as one of the most significant prior-restraint cases in history, the U.S. Supreme Court in a 6–3 decision freed the newspapers to resume publishing the material. The court held that the government had failed to justify restraint of publication.

The Pentagon Papers revealed that the Harry S. Truman administration gave military aid to France in its colonial war against the communist-led Viet Minh, thus directly involving the United States in Vietnam; that in 1954 Pres. Dwight D. Eisenhower decided to prevent a communist takeover of South Vietnam and to undermine the new communist regime of North Vietnam; that

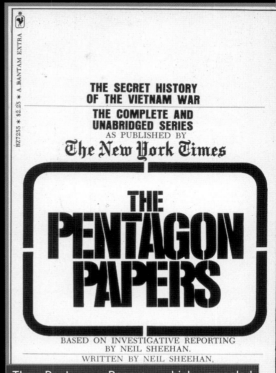

B27255 * $2.25 * A BANTAM EXTRA

THE SECRET HISTORY OF THE VIETNAM WAR

THE COMPLETE AND UNABRIDGED SERIES

AS PUBLISHED BY

The New York Times

THE PENTAGON PAPERS

BASED ON INVESTIGATIVE REPORTING BY NEIL SHEEHAN.

WRITTEN BY NEIL SHEEHAN,

The Pentagon Papers, which revealed the United States' secret military role in Indochina, were leaked in 1971 in large part because of the ease of photocopying machines.

Pres. John F. Kennedy transformed the policy of "limited-risk gamble" that he had inherited into a policy of "broad commitment"; that Pres. Lyndon B. Johnson intensified covert warfare against North Vietnam and began planning to wage overt war in 1964, a full year before the depth of U.S. involvement was publicly revealed; and that Johnson ordered the bombing of North Vietnam in 1965 despite the judgment of the U.S. intelligence community that it would not cause the North Vietnamese

Continued on page 110

Continued from page 109

to cease their support of the Viet Cong insurgency in South Vietnam.

The release of the Pentagon Papers stirred nationwide and, indeed, international controversy because it occurred after several years of growing dissent over the legal and moral justification of intensifying U.S. actions in Vietnam. The disclosures and their continued publication despite top-secret classification were embarrassing to the administration of Pres. Richard M. Nixon, who was preparing to seek reelection in 1972. So distressing were these revelations that Nixon authorized unlawful efforts to discredit Ellsberg, efforts that came to light during the investigation of the Watergate Scandal.

The papers were subsequently published in book form as *The Pentagon Papers* (1971). However, the leaked documents were incomplete, and certain portions remained classified until 2011, when the full study was released to the public.

States concluded that the Germans were no more responsible than anyone else for starting the war. Surprisingly, in 1961 a German historian, Fritz Fischer (1908–99), reopened this question with *Griff nach der Weltmacht: Die Kriegziel politik das kaiserlichen Deutschland, 1914/18* (1961; *Germany's Aims in the First World War, 1967*), kindling a lively debate in West Germany.

Comparatively little was said about the diplomacy preceding World War II—and there was little basis for saying anything—until more than the captured papers of Nazi Germany were made completely available (the British prime minister and historian Winston Churchill simply took the relevant English state papers with him when writing his six-volume history of the war). It has seemed obvious that Hitler intended to start a war, if not necessarily on September 1, 1939. But the postwar relations between the United States and the Soviet Union became the subject of controversy when the American historians William Appleman Williams (1921–90) and Gabriel Kolko (1932–2014) challenged the conventional American view that the Soviets intended world conquest and were deterred only by the North Atlantic Treaty Organization (NATO) and its nuclear umbrella. Williams and his students, who were influential in the 1960s, produced a series of revisionist accounts of the outbreak of the Korean War and later of the Vietnam War. These were in turn attacked by defenders of the orthodox view.

This sketch of the liveliest issues in postwar diplomatic history would seem to support the view of those who claim that all history is implicated in ideology. The disagreements of diplomatic historians do suggest that political and national passions play an unusually large part in their interpretation of diplomatic history. On the other hand, lack of new techniques does not mean that diplomatic historians are no better at their task than their predecessors were. Some interpretations have been definitively discredited, and signs of convergence have emerged even on such contested topics as the origins of World War I. As the European nations entered the European Union, an effort was made to write a history textbook on which historians from various countries could agree. Although it relied upon a certain amount of euphemism (the German invasion of Belgium in 1914 was referred to as a "transit" of their troops), it did show that, even in this controversial field, some consensus can be achieved.

ECONOMIC HISTORY

History and economics were once closely related. Adam Smith, Thomas Malthus, and Karl Marx were all political economists who incorporated historical data into their analyses. A historical school of economics developed in Germany in the late 19th century and was associated with figures such as Gustav von Schmoller (1838–1917). Reacting against the free-trade doctrines of British economists (which would have prevented Germany from protecting its industries until they were strong enough to compete), the historical economists argued that there are no universally valid economic laws and that each country should define its own economic path.

A similar interest in historical development was shown by institutional economists such as the eccentric genius Thorstein Veblen (1857–1929). The American Historical Association and the American Economic Association were founded together and did not separate for several years; it was common in American colleges for historians and economists to be in the same department. From the turn of the 20th century, however, the two disciplines pursued radically different paths. While economists developed ever-more-elaborate mathematical models, historians remained mired in the messy details of the world.

While this division between the disciplines occurred, much good work was done on the workings of preindustrial economies and on the question of why serfdom was introduced in Poland and Russia just as it was dying out in western Europe. In several countries, cost-of-living indexes that covered several centuries were computed. Although these estimates were imperfect (as they still are), they illuminated such famous questions as the causes of the French Revolution and the condition of the working class during the Industrial Revolution in England. The French historian Camille-Ernest Labrousse (1895–1988) showed that in France during the period from 1778 to 1789, a long recession was exacerbated by high bread prices and eventually the bankruptcy of the crown. Believers in "deeper" causes of the revolution treated this conjunction as only a trigger, but since many popular disturbances in the first years of the revolution were bread riots that turned to political violence, it is hard to avoid the conclusion that the history of the period would have been quite different under different economic conditions.

Economic history in Britain has always been influenced by the fact that it was the first country to undergo an industrial revolution. In the aftermath of World War II, economic planners looked to Britain for an example of how countries in the developing world might achieve the same transformation. The American economist and political theorist Walt Whitman Rostow (1916–2003), in *Stages of Economic Growth* (1960), attempted a general theory of how economies industrialize. His six-stage model did not gain general acceptance, but he did raise the issue of long-term economic development, which directed some economists, at least, toward history.

The proposition that the Industrial Revolution was a good thing was universally maintained by historians who were sympathetic to capitalism.

Thorstein Veblen (1857–1929), as depicted by Edwin Burrage Child

Socialist historians, on the other hand, judged it more ambivalently. For orthodox Marxists, only industrialized countries would create a proletariat strong enough to expropriate the means of production, and the enormous productive power of industrial society would be the basis of the "kingdom of plenty" under communism. At the same time, they emphasized the arbitrary way in which industrialization was carried out and the suffering of the workers. Because much of the evidence for the suffering of the workers was in fact anecdotal, a number of economic historians tried to determine whether their standard of living actually declined. Although wage rates were known, industrial workers were often laid off, so their annual income was not a simple multiple of their average wage. Despite the difficulties of the inevitably controversial calculations, it seems to be true that workers' standard of living at least did not decline, and may even have improved slightly, before 1850. This conclusion did not resolve the issue of their suffering, however, since workers also endured noneconomic losses. The matter continues to be a concern for social and economic historians.

The distinctive feature of the American economy was slavery. One overriding issue for economic historians has been whether slavery was inherently inefficient as well as inhumane and thus whether it might have disappeared through sheer unprofitability had it not been legally abolished. This is an extremely complicated question. An answer requires not only large amounts of data but also data about almost all aspects of the American economy. To see how the data fitted together, historians after World War II drew upon macroeconomic theory, which showed how various inputs affect the gross national product.

There was, however, a further problem: How did the productivity of slave labour compare with the hypothetical product of free labour applied to the same land? In other words, if there had been no slavery, would Southern agriculture have been more (or less) profitable? One attempt to resolve this counterfactual question was offered in *Railroads and American Economic Growth: Essays in Economic History* (1964) by Robert Fogel, an American economist who shared the Nobel Prize for Economics with Douglass C. North in 1993. Fogel tested the claim that railroads were of fundamental importance in American economic development by constructing a model of the American economy without railroads. The model made some simplifying assumptions: passenger travel was ignored, and since canals were the principal alternatives to railroads, the part of the United States west of the continental divide was also left out. With these provisos, the model showed that the importance of railroads had been exaggerated, because in 1890 the gross national product without railroads would have reached the same level as the actual one.

In *Time on the Cross: The Economics of American Negro Slavery*

(1974), Fogel and his colleague Stanley Engerman addressed the issue of the profitability of slavery, using the methods Fogel had developed in his earlier study. Using evidence only from the last decade of American slavery, they argued that the system was not only profitable but more profitable than free labour would have been. The response to their work illustrates many of the accomplishments and pitfalls of what came to be called cliometrics, the application of statistical analysis to the study of history. It sold more than 20,000 copies, a large number for a scholarly book; it shared the Bancroft Prize for history; and it was the subject of stories and bemused reviews in the popular press. However, because it adopted the French custom of segregating tables and other statistical matter in a second volume—which appeared not simultaneously but several months later—the initial reviewers had access only to the

Robert W. Fogel (1926–2013)

conclusions and the supporting textual arguments. These initial reviews were generally respectful, but when the second volume appeared, many cliometricians attacked its statistical analysis. Other scholars assailed the work for everything from insufficient indignation about the evils of slavery to improper attributions of classical profit-maximizing economic motives to participants in an institution that Thomas Jefferson characterized as "a continuous exercise of the most boisterous of passions." (Fogel and Engerman argued that slaves were rarely whipped because whipping would have diminished their capacity for work.)

Some of these criticisms missed the mark. Fogel and Engerman did not undertake even a political economy of slavery, much less a moral evaluation. The most searching critiques, from fellow cliometricians, were arcane and technical. But they resembled disputes in the natural sciences in that the data were publicly available, and fairly well-understood criteria were available to adjudicate the issues. Furthermore, the authors' main conclusion, which was anticipated by earlier studies, has not been refuted: Slavery was indeed profitable and was not withering on the vine in 1861.

Cliometrics was an important innovation because it offered new answers to old questions and provided a methodology better suited to tackling large questions of system and structure. Although it was a new and rather spectacular technique, it did not eclipse older branches of economic history. In the United States, which had pioneered business history, institutional historians continued their work on entrepreneurs and on management tactics, while labour history was avidly pursued not only in the United States but throughout Europe. Historians were also preoccupied by peasants in numbers sufficient to justify a Journal of Peasant Studies, and, since peasants were found all over the world, peasant studies easily became comparative. These studies readily crossed the fluid boundary between economic history and social history. Quantitative analysis of the records left by ordinary people, gathered for cliometric purposes, has brought their experiences to light—the great accomplishment of the social historians of our time.

MILITARY HISTORY

Soldiers in battle were the theme of the earliest Greek epic and the earliest histories. It has not lost its interest for modern readers and writers. The focus of academic military history, however, has changed as markedly as the nature of modern warfare has changed. The campaigns of the American Civil War, with their chesslike maneuvering and great set-piece battles, continue to fascinate, but attrition and pounding by superior force assumed an ever-greater role in 20th-century military strategy, despite yielding few brilliant generals or individual heroes. On the other hand, World War I was the first European war to be fought by literate armies, and the soldiers in that conflagration created not only a great literature but also a mass of material about their experiences. In *The Great War and Modern Memory* (1975), Paul Fussell made full use of these documents to produce an account of life in the trenches. Although the literary output of soldiers in World War II was much less significant, the American writer Studs Terkel, using techniques of oral history, managed to compile in *The Good War* (1984) a comparable panorama of its participants, including those on the home front. Perhaps the leading exponent of military history as the social history of war is John Keegan, whose work ranges from the Battle of Agincourt in 1415 to the wars of the 21st century.

POLITICAL HISTORY

For many people, and for many years, "history" simply meant political history. A large proportion of published works by historians was devoted to political history as late as the 1970s, but even before that time historians had begun to examine other topics. Although E.A. Freeman's slogan "History is past politics" no longer rings true, it is safe to say that political history will continue to be a prominent part of historical writing and will challenge the subtlety, worldly wisdom, and narrative powers of historians as long as history is written.

The primary goal of political history in the immediate postwar years was to supplement (or, in the minds of some, to supplant) the historian's traditional reliance on narrative with a scientific or quantitative approach; inevitably, this endeavour came to be called "new political history." It was to be, as William Aydelotte put it, "a sedate, hesitant, circumspect, little behavioral revolution" in American historical practice. The postwar United States furnished some innovative young historians who combined an interest in political history with a program for making it more scientific. Among the most systematic of these scholars was Lee Benson, author of an influential work that applied quantitative techniques to the study of Jacksonian democracy. "By 1984," he predicted in 1966,

a significant proportion of American historians will have accepted ... two basic propositions: (1) past human behavior can be studied scientifically; (2) the main business of historians is to participate in the overall scholarly enterprise of discovering and developing general laws of human behavior.

Wherever possible, all statements in historical works should be formulated so precisely as to be "verifiable." Implicitly but vaguely quantitative terms (e.g., most or significant proportion) should be replaced by numerical expressions.

Quantitative data to support such ambitions were available for elections. Using what he found in New York state, Benson succeeded in showing that party affiliation was largely determined by ethnic and cultural loyalties and remained surprisingly immune to the issues raised by party platforms or political speeches.

The University of Iowa was another hotbed of quantitative approaches, and electoral statistics of Iowa and other Midwestern states soon joined those of New York. The new political historians also established an archive of national election data at the University of Michigan, which they hoped to use to prepare a truly comprehensive electoral history.

Less-ambitious quantitative projects focused on parliamentary bodies. Lewis Namier (1888–1960), probably the greatest English historian of his generation, undertook the biographical study of members of Parliament. Namier borrowed the prosopographic technique of Ronald Syme, a historian of ancient Rome, which involved tracing the family connections, sources of income and influence, and offices held by a defined group of the political elite. This approach was most useful for the study of oligarchic regimes and hence was especially suitable for the Roman Senate and mid-18th-century British parliaments. The main effect of such work was to de-emphasize the impact of political ideologies and to assert the importance of kinship and personal relations in deliberative assemblies.

Sir Lewis Bernstein Namier (1888–1960)

More directly quantitative was the work of Aydelotte, who investigated the conventional claim that the English Corn Laws (protective tariffs on grain imports) were abolished because members of Parliament who represented manufacturing districts wanted the cheapest-possible food for their workers (allowing the lowest-possible wages). As plausible as this view was, significant correlations frequently failed to appear.

The new political historians carried the quantitative program into the stronghold of traditional historiography. Terms such as *impressionistic, anecdotal,* and *narrative* acquired dismissive connotations. More-traditional historians were admonished for excessive reliance on literary evidence (i.e., anything that could not be quantified).

A generation later, the debate over quantification fizzled out, leaving some permanent mark on political history. Few would now deny the value of some quantitative studies or the desirability of precision in historical language. The habit of collaboration with other historians and membership in research teams, virtually unknown earlier, is now well established. A number of intuitively obvious interpretations have been shown to be exaggerated or plainly wrong.

Nevertheless, it is clear that quantification in political history was oversold. Its idea of scientific procedures was startlingly old-fashioned, and many of the studies based solely on quantification failed to produce significant results. Sometimes things already believed were confirmed—not a useless exercise but not a high priority either. More-interesting correlations often failed the significance test or showed inexplicable relationships. Finally, attention was diverted to bodies of data that could be quantified. The most judicious of the new political historians warned against the exclusive reliance on quantification and recognized that archival research would remain indispensable, especially in the traditional fields of constitutional, administrative, and legal history.

CHAPTER EIGHT

BRANCHES OF HISTORY, PART IV: HISTORY OF SCIENCE

The history of all the branches of learning has always been a part of intellectual history, but the history of science has had a peculiarly tense relationship with it, and with history more generally. Although much history of science has been written by practicing scientists, it is almost never formally taught in science departments. It is now mostly treated as autonomous, but in some cases historians of science have been included in history faculties. Even though their relationships with other historians may be distant (though cordial), the study of the history of science is in many ways analogous to the study of other aspects of the past. The history of science has also produced, in *The Structure of Scientific Revolutions* (1962), by Thomas Kuhn (1922–96), one of the most influential books by any American historian in the postwar period. Almost everybody who uses the word paradigm in any of the many senses in which Kuhn used it is indebted to that book.

The tension between the history of ideas and intellectual history reappears in the history of science in a tension between "internalist" and "externalist" approaches to the subject.

THOMAS S. KUHN

Thomas S. Kuhn (July 18, 1922–June 17, 1996) was an American historian of science noted for *The Structure of Scientific Revolutions* (1962), one of the most influential works of history and philosophy written in the 20th century.

Kuhn earned bachelor's (1943) and master's (1946) degrees in physics at Harvard University but obtained his Ph.D. (1949) there in the history of science. He taught the history or philosophy of science at Harvard (1951–56), the University of California at Berkeley (1956–64), Princeton University (1964–79), and the Massachusetts Institute of Technology (1979–91).

In his first book, *The Copernican Revolution* (1957), Kuhn studied the development of the heliocentric theory of the solar system during the Renaissance. In his landmark second book, *The Structure of Scientific Revolutions*, he argued that scientific research and thought are defined by "paradigms," or conceptual world-views, that consist of formal theories, classic experiments, and trusted methods. Scientists typically accept a prevailing paradigm and try to extend its scope by refining theories, explaining puzzling data, and establishing more precise measures of standards and phenomena. Eventually, however, their efforts may generate insoluble theoretical problems or experimental anomalies that expose a paradigm's inadequacies or contradict it altogether. This accumulation of difficulties triggers a crisis that can only be resolved by an intellectual revolution that replaces an old paradigm with a new one. The overthrow of Ptolemaic cosmology by Copernican heliocentrism, and the displacement of Newtonian mechanics by quantum physics and general relativity, are both examples of major paradigm shifts.

Kuhn questioned the traditional conception of scientific

progress as a gradual, cumulative acquisition of knowledge based on rationally chosen experimental frameworks. Instead, he argued that the paradigm determines the kinds of experiments scientists perform, the types of questions they ask, and the problems they consider important. A shift in the paradigm alters the fundamental concepts underlying research and inspires new standards of evidence, new research techniques, and new pathways of theory and experiment that are radically incommensurate with the old ones.

Kuhn's book revolutionized the history and philosophy of science, and his concept of paradigm shifts was extended to such disciplines as political science, economics, sociology, and even to business management. Kuhn's later works were a collection of essays, *The Essential Tension* (1977), and the technical study *Black-Body Theory and the Quantum Discontinuity* (1978).

Thomas S. Kuhn, 1973

THE INTERNALIST APPROACH

To the internalist the critical questions are: What problem was the scientist attempting to solve, and how did he solve it? To answer these questions, the historian obviously needs to know in intimate detail the state of scientific thought during the time about which he is writing. But he also needs to be familiar with the nuts and bolts of scientific work—the apparatus, the experimental animals, if any, and the like. The problems for investigation are likely to be generated within the compass of what Kuhn calls "normal science," which has well-established procedures for verifying results.

The great merit of the internalist approach is also the source of its greatest difficulty. It deals with how science is actually done, which means that not many historians have the necessary knowledge of science to write it. This difficulty becomes particularly acute when modern science (roughly, science since the start of the 19th century) is the subject. The literature in the history of science is disproportionately focused on the so-called scientific revolution of the 17th century. One reason for this is that the scientific revolution was a heroic period, but another is that much less knowledge of modern science is required to understand Galileo, Johannes Kepler, or Isaac Newton than is required to understand Albert Einstein or Werner Heisenberg. Ignorance of scientific practice can be further concealed by concentrating on what scientists say about their method in the prefaces to their works. It may seem strange to make a distinction between scientific method and practice, but it is not. "Method" is not simply distilled practice, and sometimes it is a poor description of what scientists actually do. It seems clear that improvements in scientific method had relatively little to do with the successes of the scientific revolution. Furthermore, some scientific works (those of Francis Bacon, for example) are barely disguised appeals for funding, and the prefaces of others are not free of self-advertisement.

In part because a history of modern science would require knowledge of modern science, some historians who attempt the internalist mode have focused their investigations on what counted as science in the past. An influential early work in this vein, Lynn Thorndike's *A History of Magic and Experimental Science* (1923–58), discussed two seemingly distinct approaches that share the belief that human practice can affect the natural world. Distinguishing between the two approaches requires criteria—effectiveness and rationality—that are essentially modern. Sorting out what was scientific work can easily lead to a history that begins with the concepts of modern science and then looks backward to see how those categories were anticipated by earlier scientists. The result is a story of how scientists finally "got it right" after the bungling and delusions of their predecessors were corrected—though such stories inevitably tend to mangle the integrity of past scientific traditions. Another approach is to give a "rational reconstruction" of the history of science—that is, to show how the underlying logic of scientific discovery unfolded, without bothering with the irksome details of how things actually happened.

THE EXTERNALIST APPROACH

The externalist approach aims at a retrospective sociology or anthropology of scientific discovery. One of its earliest advocates was Bruno Latour, who with his colleague Steve Woolgar did fieldwork in a biological laboratory, where they discovered that scientific practice was not a pure expression of scientific method and that scientists did not disdain the use of rhetoric in reporting their results. The most aggressive partisans of this approach advocated a "strong program" for contextualizing science. Important work in contextualization has been done by Marxist

Bruno Latour

Bruno Latour (June 22, 1947–) is a French sociologist and anthropologist known for his innovative and iconoclastic work in the study of science and technology in society. Latour's early studies were in philosophy and theology, but his interests expanded to include anthropology and the philosophy of science and technology while he was stationed in Côte d'Ivoire for military service in the early 1970s. He received a doctorate in philosophy from the University of Tours in 1975.

Latour's subsequent work dealt with the activities of communities of scientists. His book *Laboratory Life* (1979), written with Steven Woolgar, a sociologist, was the result of more than a year spent observing molecular biologists at the Salk Institute for Biological Sciences in La Jolla, California. Latour and Woolgar's account broke away from the positivist view of scientific inquiry as a rational and largely asocial process capable of uncovering universally valid truths regarding the natural world. They instead presented scientific knowledge as an artificial product of various social, political, and economic interactions, most of them competitive.

Latour further expanded on these ideas in such books as *Les Microbes: guerre et paix, suivi de irréductions* (1984; published in English as *The Pasteurization of France*), *Science in Action* (1987), and *Nous n'avons jamais été modernes* (1991; *We Have Never Been Modern*). In his writings, Latour often likened the scientific community to a battlefield: new theories, facts, techniques, and technologies succeeded by marshalling enough users and supporters to overwhelm any alternatives, thus immunizing themselves against future challenges. It was by winning this fight for dominance that scientific facts came to be true; Latour dismissed questions about the universal validity of scientific facts as both unanswerable and irrelevant to his concerns. This insistence on seeing scientific facts as purely social constructions sometimes led Latour to conclusions that were seen as absurd outside the community of social theorists. In 1998, for example, Latour rejected as anachronistic the recent discovery that the pharaoh Ramses II had died of tuberculosis, asserting that the tubercle bacillus was discovered only in 1882 and could not properly be said to have existed before then.

Bruno Latour (1947–)

Another distinguishing aspect of Latour's work was its focus on the complex and heterogeneous relationships between both human and nonhuman agents. He argued that the production of scientific knowledge could be understood only by tracing networks of relationships between entities as disparate as lab animals, existing scientific texts, human researchers, experimental subjects, established technologies, and social movements, among others. This approach became known as actor-network theory, and its influence soon spread beyond Latour's field of

Continued on page 128

Continued from page 127

science and technology studies. Latour's work exasperated many practicing scientists with its denial of the existence of objective truths and its claims to have unmasked science as a social process and debunked its pretenses of rationality. However, his work was welcomed by many social scientists for its fresh and innovative approach to the study of science.

historians; their masterpiece is *Science and Civilization in China* (1954), a multivolume history of Chinese science by the English historian and scientist Joseph Needham. The traditional point of intersection between science and society is technology, and Marxist historians made valiant efforts to argue that the practical needs of ballistics influenced Newton's celestial mechanics. However, this approach is of limited usefulness for any time before the late 19th century, when chemistry revolutionized dyestuffs, pharmaceuticals, and photography; before then, science and technology had proceeded on essentially unrelated paths, accompanied by condescension from scientists and resentment from artisans. In modern times, the relationship has been much closer, and even advocates or practitioners of "pure" science often entertain the hope that some useful device will emerge.

Externalists can get by with much less scientific knowledge than internalists, which accounts for some of the appeal of the former school. Externalists have undoubtedly made clearer the process whereby people become accepted as scientists; this is vital, because there is no way to know what science is other than by knowing what the community of scientists say it is. Externalists have also shown why some topics become interesting to scientists while others are ignored. Yet natural science is probably more autonomous than most modes of knowledge production, and there are limits to how much illumination a historian can bring to the history of science without knowing a lot of science himself.

CHAPTER NINE

METHODOLOGY OF HISTORIOGRAPHY

This concluding chapter surveys contemporary historical practice and theory. As previously demonstrated, there are many branches of history today, each with different kinds of evidence, particular canons of interpretation, and distinctive conventions of writing. This diversity has led some to wonder whether the term *history* still designates an integral body of or approach to knowledge. Although the emphasis of this article falls on what historians share, it is well to remember that deviations from these norms are always lurking.

THE HISTORIAN'S SOURCES

The oldest source, oral history, is also in some ways the newest. As the emphasis of many historians has turned to social history, especially history "from the bottom up," they have had to create their own evidence through interviews with those shut out of the documentary record. Students of Victorian England have long depended on the interviews with costermongers and other street people by Henry Mayhew, the author of *London Labour and the London Poor*, 4 vol. (1851–62); without these we would not know of their attitudes toward marriage and organized religion (casual for both). One of the first great collaborative efforts in oral history was the interviews with former African American slaves conducted in the 1930s by researchers working for the Works Progress Administration (WPA). Although anyone who could remember slavery would by then have been well over 70 years old, the subsequently

These Holocaust survivors agreed to be interviewed: (first row from left) Lea Richter, Gina Ladanyi, and Raquel Sznajderhaus de Mazur, and (back row from left) Eugenia Unger and Micheline Wolanowski.

published interviews nevertheless tapped a rich vein of family stories as well as personal memories. An enterprise on a similar scale is being carried out with survivors of the Holocaust; now, however, thanks to videotaping, one can see the interviews and not merely read edited transcripts of them.

Getting permission to do an interview, and if possible to tape it, is the first task of the oral historian. Arrangements may have to be made to protect confidentiality; elaborate protocols about this have been worked out by anthropologists, which historians may emulate. People remember things that historians have no independent way of discovering; however, they also seem to remember things that did not happen or that happened quite differently. And, of course, they often fail to remember things that did happen. Correcting for the fallibility of memory is the critical task, and for this there is no substitute for preparation. An entire workweek spent preparing for a single interview is none too lavish. If the interviewer knows a good deal already, he may be able to jog or correct an otherwise recalcitrant memory or to know what is reliable and what is not. Except for the tape or video recorder, techniques for verifying oral testimony have perhaps progressed little since Thucydides.

Different techniques are required for investigating the history of peoples who adopted writing only recently. These used to be regarded as "people without history," but historians are now beginning to isolate the historical content of their oral traditions. Oral epic poetry is still being performed today, in Nigeria, Serbia, and elsewhere, and studying it not only has revealed a great deal about classical epics such as the *Iliad* but also has shown how remarkable feats of memory could be performed by trained singers of tales, preserving the memory of historical events with much less distortion than was once suspected and recovering at least some of the early history of Africa and America.

WRITTEN SOURCES

The historian confronting written documents can also draw on a long history of criticism. Manuals for beginning historians often dwell on the problem of forged documents, but this is seldom a problem, except occasionally for the medieval historian. A spectacular exception was the alleged diary of Adolf Hitler, a forgery that temporarily deceived the distinguished British historian Hugh Trevor-Roper in 1983. A more formidable challenge is simply to read well. This sometimes starts with learning to read at all. Modern advances in deciphering codes (stimulated by World War II) enabled classicists to translate Linear B, yielding evidence about the Mycenaean language used on Crete in the 2nd millennium BCE. Computerized technology promises to assist in deciphering other languages not presently understood.

Konrad Kujau (*left*) so effectively forged Hitler's diaries that renowned historian Hugh Trevor-Roper was deceived.

A much more usual problem calls for paleography—the study of ancient or medieval handwriting. Once the handwriting styles of past epochs become familiar, anything written by a professional scribe should be legible, but one can expect the wildest variations of spelling and handwriting in personal documents. Printing stabilizes texts but also leads to a long-term decline in handwriting. The British historian Lewis Namier, (1888–1960), who owed much of his success to being able to read the execrable handwriting of the duke of Newcastle, argued that the two "sciences" the historian must know are psychoanalysis and graphology.

Written documents of quite a different kind have come to prominence in social and economic history. These are administrative records

Reading

Reading is, of course, far more than making out the letters and words. Establishing the plain sense is only the first step; here the pitfalls are unrecognized technical language or terms of art. Also, the words may have changed their meaning since they were written. Furthermore, texts of any length are almost always metaphorical. Irony may be obvious (Jonathan Swift's *A Modest Proposal* was not seriously advocating raising Irish babies for the English table), but it may also be so subtle as to escape detection (did Niccolò Machiavelli really intend that his praise for Cesare Borgia be taken seriously?). What is not said is often the most important part of a text. Historians have to establish the genre to which a document belongs in order to begin to attack these hermeneutical questions (a step they sometimes omit, to their peril). Almost all English wills in the early modern period, for example, started with a bequest of the body to the graveyard and the soul to God; omission of this might be highly significant but would be noticed only if one knew what to expect from a will. The British historian G.M. Young said that the ideal historian has read so much about the people he is writing about that he knows what they will say next—a counsel of perfection, no doubt, but a goal to aspire to.

of actions that individually mean little but lend themselves to aggregation over long time spans. Social history differs from sociology, it has been said, by having "long time series and bad data." Records of dowries, baptisms, bread prices, customs receipts, or direct taxes are typical of such sources, and all of them are bad in their own way. Estimating a population by counting baptisms, for example, is hazardous if priests were negligent in keeping their registers or if the custom of baptism immediately after birth gave way to long delays between birth and baptism (giving the baby a good chance to die before the rite could be performed). Tax evasion is as ancient as taxation, and tax records as indexes of economic activity are likely to measure instead the fluctuation of mercantile honesty or effective law enforcement, not to mention the ever-present possibility that the records were poorly compiled or preserved. Cost-of-living figures are particularly difficult to compute even today and were more so in earlier periods. Records of prices paid usually come from institutions and may not be typical of what individuals bought, especially since they usually did not have to buy everything they ate or used. On the other hand, their wage rates cannot simply be multiplied by the number of hours or days in the working year, since they were seldom lucky enough not to be laid off seasonally or during recessions.

Handbooks of historical method at the end of the 19th century assured students that if they mastered the interpretation of written documents, they would have done everything required to be a historian. "No documents, no history," one said. In this century the notion of a document has been enormously expanded so that any artifact surviving from the past can serve as the answer to some historian's question. Aerial photography, for example, can reveal settlement patterns long since buried. Napoleon's hair can be examined to see whether he died a natural death or was poisoned; analysis of Newton's hair showed that he was an alchemist. The architecture along Vienna's Ringstrasse can be construed as revealing the ambitions of the liberal bourgeoisie. The history of sexuality cannot be written without the history of clothing—even the nudes in classical paintings pose in postures influenced by the clothes they are not wearing. Indeed, the ordinary things of all kinds to be found in a folk museum are one of the best sources for the everyday life of people in the past.

Artifacts do not usually tell their own stories. When written

SAMPLING

Even if historians find the evidence solid, records like this are usually too numerous not to require sampling, and drawing a truly random sample of historical records is much more complex than when doing survey research. Handbooks of statistics do not always reflect this fact. Nobody would think of undertaking a quantitative study nowadays without a computer (although desk calculators are quite adequate for some projects), and this raises a further difficulty insofar as historical records usually vary so much in terminology that they have to be encoded for computer use. Coding conventions are themselves interpretations, and few quantitative historians have never had occasion to curse themselves for premature or inconsistent coding. There is no foolproof remedy against this, but providing a database and a copy of coding conventions has become the recommended practice to enable other historians to evaluate the work.

documents can be juxtaposed to them, the results are more illuminating than either can be by themselves. Unfortunately, virtually the whole training of historians is devoted to reading written texts, so that skill is hypertrophied, while the ability to interpret material objects is underdeveloped. When historians can, for example, accurately describe how the machines of the early Industrial Revolution really worked, they will have met this challenge—which is, of course, a challenge to know almost everything.

LIBRARIES AND ARCHIVES

Historians today benefit from much more integrated and comprehensive archival and library systems than existed in previous centuries. The state papers of the United States, for example, were not in usable condition in 1933. Thanks again in part to the efforts of WPA workers, great improvements were made in cataloguing and preservation; now a new archive building in suburban Maryland has been built to cope with the tide of documents produced by the U.S. government. The same step has been taken in Britain, and both Britain and France have new national libraries. Less spectacular, but invaluable to many historians, are the local historical societies, county record offices, and the like, which have been established in many countries. These have allowed the collection and preservation of documents that originated in a great variety of places—churches, courts, city and county governments, legal offices, and collections of letters. One of the remarkable developments of the period since the dissolution of the

The Library of Congress Packard Campus for Audio-Visual Conservation is home to 6.3 million items, for which there is state-of-the-art storage.

Soviet Union in 1991 has been the widespread sale of public and private records to Western collectors. Libraries such as Yale or the Hoover Institution (at Stanford University) are now in many ways better places to study the Soviet period than any in Russia, and if one can fault the failure of the Russian government to pay its librarians and the wild capitalism of the new Russia for dispersing these treasures, at least they will be safely preserved. They have already answered many questions about how the Soviet Union was run.

The proliferation of libraries and archives illustrates what is in some ways the greatest difficulty with regard to modern sources—there are too many of them. Most discussions of historiography focus on how historians tease out the exiguous meanings of documents when they are very scarce. The problem facing the historian of the 19th century and even more of the 20th is how to cope with the vast array sources open to him. Computers and the Internet have vastly enhanced the speed with which printed sources can be searched—titles of all the books in all the major Western libraries are online—but the historian must know a great many descriptors to do a reasonable subject search. Furthermore, the Internet has brought as much misinformation as information, if not more.

In the 16th and 17th centuries it was taken for granted that the historian would work alone and would usually own many of his books. The library of Göttingen, the pride of 18th-century Germany, would be small even for a new university or a modest liberal-arts college today. Great reputations could be made in the 19th century for the discovery of a new archive (such as Ranke's discovery of the Venetian *relazioni*). Nothing like this could possibly happen today, yet such is the conservatism of the historical profession that the model is still the single scholar exhausting the archives. The archives for modern history are inexhaustible, and collaboratively written works, already becoming somewhat common, will almost certainly have to become even more so if historians are to meet their traditional goals of comprehensive research.

FROM EXPLANATION TO INTERPRETATION

Until quite recently almost everybody who thought about historiography focused on the historian's struggle with the sources. Philosophers were interested in the grounds they had for claiming to make true statements about the past. This directed their attention to the process of research; it was not unusual to say that after learning "what actually happened," the historian then faced only the relatively unproblematic process of "writing up" his findings. This emphasis aptly captured the way that historical method is taught and the understanding of their craft (as they like to call it) that historians entertain. Nevertheless, no historian can rest content simply with establishing facts and setting them forth in chronological order. Histories, as opposed to annals and chronicles, must not only establish what happened but also explain why it happened and interpret the significance of the happening.

The slightest familiarity with historical writing shows that historians believe that they are explaining past events. Criticizing the explanations presented by other historians is an integral part of historical scholarship—sometimes carried to such tedious lengths that the actual narrative of events disappears under a tissue of scholastic sludge. However, it is unusual for historians to question what constitutes a historical explanation. A few abnormally reflective ones—and those few philosophers who have turned their attention to thinking about history—have demonstrated that this is not a simple task.

One philosophical school, logical positivism (also called logical empiricism), held that all other scholarly disciplines should offer explanations like those of physics, the most advanced (and mathematicized) science. The model of historical explanation was illustrated by the bursting of the radiator in an automobile. Explanation of this mishap went as follows: first, certain "boundary conditions" have to be specified—the radiator was made of iron and filled with water without antifreeze, and the car was left in the driveway when the temperature fell below freezing. The explanation consists in enumerating the relevant boundary conditions and then adducing the appropriate "covering" laws—in this case, that water expands as it freezes and the tensile strength of iron makes it too brittle to expand as much as the water does. These are, of course, laws of physics, not of history.

This certainly explains why the radiator of this car burst; such things always happen when a radiator full of water without antifreeze is exposed to subfreezing weather. Scientific explanations are also predictions: "why?" also means "on what occasions?" But is this a historical explanation? A historian would want to go well beyond it; for him the real question would be why the owner exposed the car in this manner. Was he unaware of what happens to unprotected cars in such temperatures? Unlikely. Did he, wrongly, think that he had put antifreeze in the car? Or was he misled by a faulty weather forecast?

Questions like these made historians disinclined to accept this as an example of a satisfactory historical explanation. The author of the example, the philosopher Carl Hempel, granted as much. As he understood, historians do not explain but give "explanation sketches" that have to be filled out before they attain that dignity. One prodigious difficulty is that no covering laws of history have been discovered. One candidate for such a law is, "Whenever two armies, one much larger than the other but equally well led, meet in battle, the larger one always prevails." The difficulty with this is that there are no independent standards for evaluating leadership. There are examples of much smaller armies beating larger ones, and one counterexample is enough to disconfirm a law. If one tries to save the law by saying that, in those cases, the armies were not equally well led, the argument becomes circular. Another candidate for a historical law is, "Full employment and stable prices cannot exist at the same time." Some would argue that these supposedly incompatible conditions were achieved in the U.S. economy in 1997. It all depends on how full employment is defined. It is an additional complication that this law, if it is a law, may be restricted in its application to capitalism.

For many years the lack of well-warranted covering laws seemed to be the chief difficulty with this conception of historical explanation, but chaos theory has recently raised another problem: the boundary conditions cannot be exactly specified. Even a minute and imperceptible variation in the original state of a system may have large and entirely unpredictable consequences at some time in its future state. (This is picturesquely dramatized in the image of a butterfly sneezing in Africa and the ensuing hurricane in Florida.)

Hempel subsequently modified his position by substituting high probabilities for invariable laws. In other words, an event might be explained by showing that, under these conditions, the outcome was what usually or almost always happened. This maneuver gave up the ideal of the unity of scientific explanation—that explanation in history would have the same logical structure as that in physics—because showing what almost always happens does not explain why, for this particular event, the outcome was the more- rather than the less-usual one. On the other hand, many generalizations in history have a high degree of probability but are not certain—including the likely result of going into battle with far inferior forces. It is also highly useful to know whether outcomes were almost certainly going to occur or whether they were complete surprises. And it is worthwhile trying to discover more such generalizations.

Such generalizations in fact play an important part in the other principal account of historical explanation, which focuses on the reasoning processes and intentions of historical actors. This approach is more congenial to historians than the one that attempts to work with historical laws, and it has been formulated by philosophers who were either historians themselves (R.G. Collingwood) or particularly acquainted with historical work (William Dray and Louis Mink). Its classic statement, by Collingwood, was that the historian's "why?" is not "on what occasions?" but "what did he think, that made him do it?" Collingwood believed that the historian could rethink the thoughts of the actor (as one can work out the same geometrical reasoning as Pythagoras); thus, historical knowledge could be based on a kind of acquaintance. Although Collingwood did not discount the presence of irrational elements in historical action, other historians put more emphasis on understanding these elements through empathy or intuition.

It is difficult for explanations of this kind to avoid a kind of circularity. People deliberating on an action usually have reasons to do more than one thing, and they are very seldom in the habit of leaving a written record of their deliberations. Consequently, the historian almost always has to work backward, from what was done to the reasons for doing it. But the evidence that these were the reasons for doing it is that it was done. So what is supposed to explain an action is instead explained by it. The "logic of the situation"—showing that, under the circumstances, what was done was the right or reasonable thing to do—is commonly advanced as an explanation by historians, and it can undoubtedly be convincing if one is not too fussy about what constitutes an explanation. But this means that the explanation is plausible or persuasive, not logically compelling—in other words, it signals a shift toward rhetoric.

Most of what philosophers and historians have thought about explanation has centered on how to explain single events or actions. History, however, is about far more than these, and historical writing in the 20th century moved steadily away from emphasizing individual action and toward the history of large-scale social structures. Furthermore, history is not composed of well-thought-out actions that accomplish their goals; it is instead full of the unintended consequences of actions. These result from social processes that obviously were not anticipated or understood by the actor. While the existence of unintended outcomes obviously poses insuperable difficulties for explanations in terms of individual intentions, it is exactly what theories of universal history are equipped to explain. The first articulation of the providential theory, Genesis 50:20, shows that Joseph's envious brothers had inadvertently performed God's will when they sold him into slavery, since he rose to high office in Egypt, managed the food supply so as to avert famine, and so had food to give his brothers. As Joseph says to them, "You meant evil against me; but God meant it for good, to bring it about that many people should be kept alive."

In a similar vein, Vico's "rational civil theology" recognizes that "men have themselves made this world of nations" but goes on to assert that "this world without doubt has issued from a mind often diverse, at times quite contrary, and always superior to the particular ends that men had proposed to themselves, which narrow ends, made means to serve wider ends, it has always employed to preserve the human race upon this earth." Intending just to gratify lust, humans create the institution of marriage; intending to exert power over others, they wind up with civil laws.

Much the same argument can be found in Adam Smith's notion of the invisible hand, which produces for society the optimum distribution of goods even though *homo economicus* acts totally selfishly. Hegel's great men, or world-historical individuals, such as Alexander the Great and Napoleon, are similarly moved only by ambition, but the result of their actions furthers the development of Spirit in spreading Greek culture and a rational code of law. Hegel calls this the "cunning of Reason." Finally, for Marx, individual capitalists, and the bourgeoisie as a class, act only to increase their power and perpetuate their profits, but the result of their actions is inevitably to increase the number and misery of the proletarians who will eventually overthrow them.

Theories like this necessarily suggest that history is being made behind the backs (or over the heads) of actual humans, since they cannot "make history" by achieving the goals of their actions. It appears that some sort of commitment of faith is required to accept one of these master narratives. God, or a cosmic teleology, is the ultimate explanation of everything, which means that there is nothing that cannot be explained in those terms. Logicians, however, say that universal explanations are vacuous, since nothing could happen that would show that the explanatory principle was inapplicable.

There are thus serious difficulties with explanation by laws, by intentions, or by appeal to providence or teleology. If historians believe they are explaining things, it might be that they pay little attention to these philosophical arguments, or it might be that they tacitly abandon the goal of giving a logically compelling explanation and settle for one that is highly plausible. A third possibility is that they looked in the wrong place for a warrant for their explanations. Perhaps they should have looked to the explanatory power of narratives.

NARRATIVES

During the ascendancy of social-scientific approaches to history, narratives acquired a bad name. The term suggested the logical fallacy *post hoc ergo propter hoc*—the belief that simply arranging things in chronological order proved a causal sequence. As the quantifiers suffered various reverses, some of their old supporters moved back to the claim that constructing a narrative was essential to the historian's activity and that narratives could convey understanding of the past in a distinctive fashion. If so, the autonomy of history as a discipline could be defended against the charge that it was a defective science.

During the 1970s in particular, there was a surge of interest in narrative throughout the human sciences, including anthropology, psychology, and sociology. Literary critics developed "narratology," the systematic study of narratives, especially novels and histories. In the process they greatly enriched the simple Aristotelian notion of narratives, making it possible to see that many histories, including quantitative ones, were narratives that achieved their persuasive effects in part because they were narratives. Many features of historical interpretation could be understood as properties of narratives. The choice of central subject, the decision as to when to begin and when to end the story, the characterization of the principal actors, the drawing out of moral import, and the identification of turning points are all activities that both historians and novelists perform.

The cogency of the analysis of historical narrative was enhanced by emphasizing that historians use ordinary language. Although they may borrow technical words from other disciplines, they are committed to words such as so, hence, thus, and therefore and hence to the causal linkages that these words imply. Similarly, there is no way to purge ordinary language of its normative connotations. It is therefore vain to dream of a value-free historiography or one free of any causal inferences.

One might expect the rehabilitation of narrative, even more than the emphasis on explanation through intentions of the actors, to give historians a sense that theoreticians of history were finally attending carefully to actual historical practice. As it turned out, the reaction of historians was less than enthusiastic. Narrative might convey understanding, but its advocates usually avoided using words such as explanation. There seemed to be no way for explanations to be anything more than highly plausible.

Insofar as histories interpret rather than explain, there appears to be no way to escape a relativism that would qualify, if not altogether subvert, any claim that histories are true. Proposed explanations can be contrasted and argued about, with the aim of reaching the true explanation; interpretations can be more or less plausible, deep, or ingenious but not true to the exclusion of every other possible interpretation. In the construction of narrative, Hayden White pointed out, a fictive element is inevitably introduced. The historical narrative should consist only of true statements (that is, those most consonant with the appropriate evidence), but in making them into a narrative the historian draws on the same sorts of plots and metaphors that are common to generic narratives. Their readers are prepared to believe them not just because they accept that all the individual statements are true but also because they respond to the story elements common to their culture. Making an even more relativistic claim, White argued that the same set of events could be worked up into different histories, each containing nothing but true statements and thus not vulnerable on empirical grounds but informed by different tropes and "emplotted" in a variety of ways. What looked to one historian like a comedy might seem to another a romance. His position was not that no one true history could be written—the extreme skeptical view of René Descartes—but that a variety of true histories could be written about the same events. This variety is inevitable in the absence of an acceptable master narrative, which would allow stories to be fitted together so as to make them episodes in one overarching narrative.

ART OR SCIENCE?

For generations historians have posed this rather silly question: Is history an art or a science? Usually the comforting answer has been: Both. But in the late 20th century critics said: Neither. History certainly does not meet the criteria for being called a science in the rigorous sense of the word common in the Anglo-Saxon world. It has no laws, no essential use of mathematics, and no technical language that might stand in for mathematics. In the more lenient definition of science (*scienza, Wissenschaft*) found in Continental languages, it is, because it has a recognizable body of practitioners and generally accepted protocols for validating its claims to truth. The story of how these have developed has taken up much of this article, and there is no reason to downplay their usefulness. But one should not ask too much of history; it cannot be, as many 19th-century thinkers hoped, the master science. Before placing that crown on some other discipline (anthropology, say, or biology), however, a careful study of their epistemological problems and pretensions should be made.

PRESENTATION OF HISTORY

This theme naturally leads to an exploration of the artistic elements in history. It is as naive to think of the historian merely writing up findings as to picture him handing over facts to the sociologist to be allocated to the proper laws. Some idea of the literary forms that history might take are present throughout the research process, but they are also to a degree controlled by that process.

Although Aristotle said that it made no difference to the essence of a history whether it was in prose or in verse, no truly historical epic poem has ever been written. Historians do not even go in for ballads, nor is one likely to see them trying their hands at history painting or writing librettos for operas. The vast majority of historical writing will thus be discursive prose works, though the chance that some of their words may be performed by actors is greater now than it once was.

Writing with wit and elegance is like moving with speed for an athlete—it cannot be coached. Anyone, however, can learn to write clear, plain prose. Luckily, that is what colleagues and even the general public expect from historians. Besides mastering the rules that books—or computer programs—recommend for this style, such as avoiding passive verbs, substituting short or at least Germanic for Latinate words where possible, and the like, there are some problems peculiar to historical writing.

One is how much of the sources to quote. The American historian Jack Hexter wrote entertainingly about this issue, pointing out that excessive quotation breaks up the flow of the narrative and introduces discordant voices into the text. Instead, there are times when a point can be made only with the exact words of a source. There is no rule that shows where the happy medium lies, and this is one of the facts that justify calling history a craft. Another case for tact and discrimination is the use of footnotes. Here good writers recommend not showing off. The reader is entitled to some way of seeing how accurately the historian has interpreted—or quoted—the evidence, but footnotes should not be overlong and in particular should not be converted into minibibliographies, especially when these have as one purpose to show how many books and articles the historian has read (or wants to persuade the reader that he has read).

Of course the historian should write accurately, but this is not a simple matter. Lack of a technical vocabulary is often interpreted as a defect of history, but it need not be so. Quantitative findings, for example, look more "scientific" if they are presented as percentages, but besides the necessity to present some measure giving variation from central tendency, such as standard deviations, very few historical sources lend themselves to the sort of accuracy that makes 63.8 percent any more accurate than nearly two-thirds. Wherever possible, quantitative series should be presented graphically; nothing is drearier, as Hexter notes, than attempting to write out a series of numbers in prose. The moral judgments and causal statements in historical writing are also criticized as vague, but they may be precise enough for ambiguous situations, where moral responsibility may be distributed among a number of agents or the precise relationship between causes and preconditions is tangled. Historians can take heart from the failure of translation machines to cope with all the nuances possible in natural languages.

So advice about how to write history is readily available, but historians may lack motivation. The reward structure of the profession certainly affords few incentives to learn good writing. Graduate training overwhelmingly concentrates on research techniques; courses in writing for historians are rare and almost never compulsory. The other guarantor of literary quality, copyediting, is becoming a lost art. Most historians today write mainly or only for other historians. To be qualified for lifetime employment, a historian must produce works of original research—as many as possible—that are favorably evaluated by peers. They may not prize literary skill very highly in comparison with demonstrated mastery of the sources, and they already know many things that would have to be explained to general readers.

It is increasingly expected that a young historian in search of a tenured teaching position will publish not only a first book, based on a doctoral thesis, but also a second and usually more ambitious one. In this respect American universities are beginning to approximate the expectation of two theses long common in French and German ones.

Insistence on early and copious production militates against choosing themes of general interest, because it takes much longer to write books about those. The professionalization of history and the invariably accompanying division of labor have also meant that historians focus on smaller segments of the historical record. Nor are they immune to the lure of the "MPU," or minimum publishable unit—the smallest bit of a project that an editor will accept and that, duly noted in a curriculum vitae, will reassure department chairs or funding agencies of one's continuing scholarly vitality.

Collaborative research may be one remedy against this tendency to know more and more about less and less, but collaborative writing, absent divine aid, is unlikely to achieve outstanding literary merit. (According to legend, the 70 translators of the Hebrew Bible into Greek all came up with identical texts; the only example of a great literary work done by committee is the King James translation of the Bible.)

NAVIGATING THE PARADOX

Historians consequently find themselves in a paradoxical position. Public interest in the past has seldom been higher. Some is in the nostalgic mode, and this can be expected to increase as the percentage of elderly people in the population rises. Some is in the service of political agendas, sometimes for entirely understandable reasons; for example, Jews are determined that nobody forget the Holocaust, and defenders of capitalism will continue to note that the Soviet experiment turned out badly. In addition, now that it is customary for everyone to call his ethnic background a "heritage," the commemoration and celebration of ancestors is a growth industry.

One of the more bizarre manifestations of historical interest has been the apology. The prime minister of Britain, for example, apologized for the inaction of Britain during the great Irish famine, and the pope apologized for the 16th-century St. Bartholomew's Day massacre (actually committed by the French monarch).

Interest in history also benefits from the insatiable demand of the media for "product," which has vastly strained the capacity of writers to meet it with purely invented materials. Thus, the "docudrama," "nonfiction novel," and television miniseries "based on a true story" have proliferated to supplement the flagging imaginations of the fabulators. All this has been going on while interest in academic history appears to be declining, if figures for undergraduate enrollments or academic appointments are a fair indicator.

This paradox is both a challenge and an opportunity for academic historians. They are unlikely to see a repetition of the publishing success of Thomas Macaulay's *History of England* (1849–61)—sig-

Marc Bloch (1886–1944)

nificantly, not by a professional historian—but the capacity to write for the general public is not intrinsically incompatible with holding university appointments.

The challenge to historical writing for a wider readership is clear. Few historians are taught to do it; many feel they do not need to do it; and professional rewards are not given for doing it. Yet some historians are not content to leave presentation of accounts of the past to novelists and filmmakers and are responding to some of the opportunities presented by the public interest in history. Some of them are relaxing the conventions of historical writing in the interests of greater liveliness. Historians are taught, for example, never to use first-person singular or second-person pronouns. By banishing "I"—"the most disgusting pronoun," according

149

DIALOGUE

The ability to create convincing dialogue for historical characters is essential to creators of historical plays, movies, and television series. These creators have often, for historians, been all too creative—though even the fantasies of some modern movies are models of accuracy compared with some famous historical plays. (In Friedrich von Schiller's *Maid of Orleans,* for example, Joan of Arc dies in battle.) In the 1990s an American cable channel showed films about the past with commentary afterward from a panel of historians, who usually pointed out what liberties had been taken with the historical record rather than criticizing the aesthetic impact of the film. Obviously, a more satisfactory solution would be for historians to be more proactive. Natalie Zemon Davis served as the historical counselor for a movie version of the Martin Guerre story. Her services were not confined merely to ascertaining the authenticity of the props—something Hollywood studios were quite meticulous about—but extended to working with the actors on their characterizations and with the director on the plot. French directors have often worked with historical counselors; it is a practice that would improve the historical literacy of American audiences.

to Gibbon—from the text, the historian can make it appear that an omniscient observer has written it. The great Marc Bloch, however, advocated bringing the reader into the research process by recounting the difficulties and occasional triumphs that the author experienced, not only helping to signal what is well-grounded and what is more speculative but also, if well done, sharing some of the puzzle-solving excitement that inspires people to be historians in the first place.

Another convention, in place only since the professionalization in the 19th century, forbids historians to quote anything but the actual words spoken by their subjects. Even the invented speeches of Thucydides, so scrupulously identified as such, fell under this ban. However, Garrett Mattingly (1900–62), generally regarded as the master of historical narrative among American historians, enlivened his work with speeches he wrote and attributed to historical characters—without always identifying them as invented. Other historians are now following his example. The results have not always been happy, because writing convincing dialogue is difficult, but since historians often claim to re-create the inner thoughts of people they are writing about, creating dialogue for them is no more speculative than creating indirect speech.

TECHNOLOGY AND THE 21ST CENTURY

The technological advances of the 21st century will undoubtedly bring new opportunities for the presentation of history. In the early 2000s there was already an interactive video game whose premise was that an evil woman has torn out the pages of the book in which human history is inscribed and substituted false information for them. The player, armed with a reference work, must replace the falsehoods with the correct information supplied by that work. The game is an apt allegory. Time itself has done its best to efface knowledge of the human past and has allowed ideologically distorted versions of that past to flourish instead. The historian's task is to defeat time and the loss or deceits of memory. Unfortunately, there is no data bank of infallible truths to which one can have recourse—but that simply means that the game is never over.

There may come a time when it no longer seems worth playing, as some postmodernist thinkers have suggested—though postmodernism defines itself as post through a historical judgment. Historical thought, turned on itself, shows that history has not always existed, nor is it found in every culture. Historians, of all people, are reluctant to pose as prophets because they know best how various are the twists and turns of human events. It is therefore impossible to find a conclusive argument against the suggestion of Foucault that history, like the human subject, will prove to be a transitory conception.

Postmodernism taught that texts allow many interpretations and that there is nothing other than the text. Its attacks on "essentialism" made it much harder to use "history" in such a way as to attribute will or agency to it, or even a capacity to teach. (Here Hegel had anticipated this position by saying that all one can learn from history is that humans have never learned from history.) Historians cannot make the grandiose claims for their discipline that were credible in the 19th century. Nevertheless, they know that there was a Holocaust, and they know that, despite Joseph Stalin's efforts to make him an "unperson," Leon Trotsky played some role in the Russian Revolution. Also, it makes quite a difference whether there was a Holocaust or not. This is reducing the case against total relativism or constructivism to truisms, but truisms are nonetheless true. It is hard to imagine that humanity's grasp of the past, so laboriously achieved and tenuous as it is, would lightly be loosened.

CONCLUSION

As discussed in this book, historiography is the activity and craft of writing history. The term also refers to written works of history and to the theory and history of historical writing. There is a difference between the past, and the history of the past. The past is simply the people who lived and the events that took place during previous times. History, however, is the way that historians look at those events and people and interpret them. The interpretations can vary considerably because they are subject to the perspective or focus with which the historian has viewed that moment in time, what the historian brings to that focus, and what framework he or she constructs around it. History is not a concrete set of unchanging facts; instead, it is an ongoing discussion that changes constantly. Historiography, in one sense of the term, is the study of this discussion, of how historians have brought their own particular focus or perspective to their research, including that derived from the branch or branches of historical study in which they specialize. History is a living, breathing subject, and historiography explores it through all the perspectives that make it so diverse.

BESTIARY A medieval often illustrated work in verse or prose describing with an allegorical moralizing commentary the appearance and habits of real and fabled animals.

CALIPH A Muslim political leader claiming rightful succession to the caliphate, the Muslim state in the centuries after the death of the Prophet Muhammad in 632 CE.

DECONSTRUCTION A form of philosophical and literary analysis that questions the fundamental conceptual distinctions of Western philosophy through a close examination of the language and logic of philosophical and literary texts.

EMPIRICISM The theory associated especially with the British philosophers John Locke, George Berkeley, and David Hume that almost all knowledge originates in experience.

EPOCH An event or a time marked by an event that begins a new period or development; a new beginning.

HAGIOGRAPHY The writing of the lives of saints.

HEGEMONY Dominant influence or authority especially of one nation over others.

HELIOCENTRIC Referred to or measured from the sun's center or appearing as if seen from it; having or relating to the sun as the center (as of the planetary system).

INSUPERABLE Incapable of being surmounted, such as incapable of being vanquished.

LOGOGRAPHER A prose writer in ancient Greece.

PARADIGM A model pattern.

PARADOX A statement that seems to contradict common sense or itself and yet is or may be true.

PHILOSOPHE Any of the writers, scientists, and thinkers of 18th-century France who were united, in spite of divergent personal views, in their conviction of the supremacy and efficacy of human reason.

POLYMATH One of encyclopedic learning.

RELATIVISM A theory that knowledge is relative to the limited nature of the mind and the conditions of knowing.

SKEPTICISM The philosophical doctrine that true and absolute knowledge is unattainable.

VICISSITUDE A change or succession from one thing to another.

ZEITGEIST The general intellectual, moral, and cultural state of an era.

Michael Bentley, *Modern Historiography* (1999), is a fine introduction. Herbert Butterfield, *Man on His Past* (1955, reissued 1969), describes the achievement of technical skills by the historians of 18th- and 19th-century Germany, while his posthumous *The Origins of History*, ed. by Adam Watson (1981), addresses, among other things, the question of why historical thought arose in some ancient cultures and not in others.

There is no substitute for reading complete historical works, but their flavour at least can be found in various anthologies. Donald R. Kelley (ed.), *Versions of History from Antiquity to the Enlightenment* (1991), gives samples of western European historical writing through the 18th century.

HISTORY OF HISTORIOGRAPHY

Historiography of a sort, like much else, can be traced to ancient Mesopotamia, as argued in Samuel Noah Kramer, *From the Tablets of Sumer* (1956, reissued as *History Begins at Sumer*, 1988), which also treats other aspects of Sumerian society. Historical writing in China is similarly ancient; a good guide is Charles S. Gardner, *Chinese Traditional Historiography* (1938, reissued 1966).

There is a vast body of scholarship on the Classical Greek and Roman historians, but almost all of it can be found by any bibliographical search for works on individual historians. Arnaldo Momigliano, *Studies in Historiography* (1966, reissued 1985), and *The Classical Foundations of Modern Historiography* (1990), are collections of essays and lectures by one of the greatest historians of historiography. Less familiar in the West is the rich Muslim tradition of historiography, which is the subject of Franz Rosenthal, *A History of Muslim Historiography*, 2nd rev. ed. (1968).

Beryl Smalley, *Historians in the Middle Ages* (1974), is an accessible and well-illustrated sketch of medieval historiography in all parts of

Europe. One of the earliest works to take an interest in the relationship of memory to history is Janet Coleman, *Ancient and Medieval Memories* (1992, reissued 2005).

Two huge books give encyclopaedic treatment to historians in the Renaissance: Eric Cochrane, *Historians and Historiography in the Italian Renaissance* (1981); and Constanin Fasolt, *The Limits of History* (2004).

Many authors treat the national historiographical traditions that were beginning to be established in the 16th century. Anthony Grafton, *What Was History?: The Art of History in Early Modern Europe* (2007), emphasizes the literary character of that historiography, and his *Defenders of the Text: The Traditions of Scholarship in an Age of Science, 1450–1800* (1991), discusses the challenges presented to it.

Not surprisingly, there is an enormous body of literature about the development of German professional historiography in the 18th and 19th centuries. Georg G. Iggers, *The German Conception of History: The National Tradition of Historical Thought from Herder to the Present*, rev. ed. (1983), retains its importance. On the German Enlightenment, the best study is Peter Hanns Reill, *The German Enlightenment and the Rise of Historicism* (1975). Jörn Rüsen (ed.), *Meaning and Representation in History* (2006), is an extensive study of German historical scholarship and historical theory.

One of the best ways to approach the lively current American historiographical scene is through Gordon S. Wood, *The Purpose of the Past: Reflections on the Uses of History* (2008), a wide-ranging collection of thoughtful review essays. John Higham, *History: Professional Scholarship in America*, updated ed. (1989), is a comprehensive discussion of 20th-century scholarship.

The essays in Paul Gordon Lauren (ed.), *Diplomacy: New Approaches in History, Theory, and Policy* (1979), give a good introduction to the issues that arise in diplomatic history. Reasons to study diplomatic history are suggested in Richard E. Neustadt and Ernest R. May, *Thinking in Time: The Uses of History for Decision-Makers* (1986).

BIOGRAPHY AND PSYCHOHISTORY

The nearest thing to a theory of biography is presented in Leon Edel, *Writing Lives: Principia Biographica* (1984). The essays in William McKinley Runyan (ed.), *Psychology and Historical Interpretation* (1988), set forth the main issues, and his *Life Histories and Psychobiography* (1982), is an excellent treatment of how to evaluate alternative explanations of events in a life history (such as Van Gogh's surgery on his own ear).

Biographies of course readily become psychohistories. The best case for the view that historians should appropriate psychoanalytic theory is made in Peter Gay, *Freud for Historians* (1985); the case against is made in David E. Stannard, *Shrinking History: On Freud and the Failure of Psychohistory* (1980).

A development of psychohistory that brings it into the history of mentalités is the upsurge of interest in memory as historical reflection. Pierre Nora, *Realms of Memory: Rethinking the French Past*, ed. by Lawrence D. Kritzman, 3 vol. (1996–98), and *Rethinking France* (2001–), are both translations of the original French classic, which began publication in 1984.

ECONOMIC HISTORY

A nontechnical and amiable approach to the accomplishments and limitations of the "new history," or "cliometrics," is Robert William Fogel and G.R. Elton, *Which Road to the Past?: Two Views of History* (1983). The logic of explanation in economic history is convincingly explicated in Peter D. McClelland, *Causal Explanation and Model Building in History, Economics, and the New Economic History* (1975).

SOCIAL AND CULTURAL HISTORY

Any history of postwar historiography will necessarily have much to say about social history, but its theoretical underpinnings are less frequently discussed. Despite its title, Philip Abrams, *Historical Sociology* (1982), is highly pertinent to social history, since Abrams argues for dissolving the boundaries between the two. Arthur L. Stinchcombe, *Theoretical Methods in Social History* (1978), takes the sharply different position that social theory is not applicable to history but that history can be used to develop social theory.

Cultural history has now taken the spotlight that shone on social history a generation earlier. Two collections of essays make the best introduction to it: Roger Chartier, *Cultural History: Between Practices and Representations*, trans. by Lydia G. Cochrane (1988), particularly good on the history of *mentalités* and well informed about American and German work; and Lynn Hunt (ed.), *The New Cultural History* (1989), focusing especially on how methods of literary criticism assist in "reading" social phenomena as texts.

WOMEN'S HISTORY

Besides its intrinsic interest and importance, women's history—because it has developed almost entirely since the end of World War II—offers a particularly clear example of how historical scholarship has changed. Its seminal work is Simone de Beauvior, *The Second Sex*, ed. and trans. by H.M. Parshley (1952). Gerda Lerner, *The Majority Finds Its Past: Placing Women in History* (1979, reissued 2005), by one of the earliest American practitioners of women's history, takes stock of the developing field. The experience of women in the developing world is illuminated by the essays in Cheryl Johnson-Odim and Margaret Strobel (eds.), *Expanding the Boundaries of Women's History* (1992).

INTELLECTUAL HISTORY

Like psychohistory, intellectual history (not quite the same thing as the history of ideas) has generated a large theoretical and methodological literature. It also has its own history in Donald R. Kelley, *The Descent of Ideas: The History of Intellectual History* (2002). George Boas, *The History of Ideas* (1969), is an introduction by an eminent practitioner.

Most intellectual historians have traditionally proceeded on the assumption that their first, if not their only, job was to discover the intentions of the authors of the texts they study; Mark Bevir, *The Logic of the History of Ideas* (1999), defends a modest form of this practice. The most persuasive statement of the view that writers never say entirely clearly what they mean because they need to evade censorship or self-censorship is Leo Strauss, *Persecution and the Art of Writing* (1952, reprinted 1988). Dominick LaCapra, *Rethinking Intellectual History: Texts, Contexts, Language* (1983), is a collection of essays by the most vocal critic of the "intentionalist" approach.

HISTORY OF SCIENCE

Thomas S. Kuhn, *The Structure of Scientific Revolutions*, 3rd ed. (1996), was almost an instant classic when it first appeared in 1962, forcing its author to spend much of the rest of his life explaining exactly what he meant. Many philosophers of science have undertaken to correct the misunderstandings (as they see them) of historians; a characteristic example is Joseph Agassi, *Towards an Historiography of Science* (1963), written from the perspective of Karl Popper.

HISTORIES OF ART AND LITERATURE

Historians of the visual arts have been unusually agitated about a "crisis" in art history, perhaps disturbed by the argument first made in Arthur C. Danto, *The Transfiguration of the Commonplace* (1981), that art itself is at an end. Two subsequent books worry over this perceived crisis: Hans Belting, *The End of the History of Art?* (1987; originally published in German, 1983); and Donald Preziosi, *Rethinking Art History: Meditations on a Coy Science* (1989).

The moving image has begun to attract the attention of historians, which surely will increase. Notable treatments are Paul Smith (ed.), *The Historian and Film* (1976, reissued 2008); John E. O'Connor (ed.), *Image as Artifact: The Historical Analysis of Film and Television* (1990); and Richard Francaviglia and John Rodnitzky (eds.), *Lights, Camera, History: Portraying the Past in Film* (2007).

Literary criticism and historiography have drawn closer together. Robert Hodge, *Literature as Discourse: Textual Strategies in English and History* (1990), is mostly for students of English but does discuss realistic fiction as a historical source and the ways in which histories and literature should interact. Brook Thomas, *The New Historicism: And Other Old-Fashioned Topics* (1991), is a sympathetic though not uncritical account of both new and old in literary studies.

WORLD HISTORY

There is nothing in principle that cannot be included under the rubric "world history," which means that it risks being a catch-all category for every subject of scholarly investigation that does not fit under a national or period designation. This is why there are shades of difference in the phrases "global history" (emphasizing globalization and economic re-lationships) and "international history," which in turn shades into dip-lomatic history. A fine introduction is David Christian, *Maps of Time: An Introduction to Big History* (2004). On the university level world his-tory is being vigorously developed, as can be seen in Bruce Mazlish and Ralph Buultjens (eds.), *Conceptualizing Global History* (1993, reissued 2004); and Philip Pomper, Richard H. Elphick, and Richard T. Vann (eds.), *World History: Ideologies, Structures, and Identities* (1998).

NONWESTERN HISTORIOGRAPHY

Much modern historical writing outside Europe and North America is naturally published in non-European languages, and many more works in European languages are translated into these languages than from them. There are, however, a growing number of informative works in English. Examples are Youssef M. Choueiri, *Modern Arab Historiogra-phy: Historical Discourse and the Nation-State*, rev. ed. (2003); Michael Gottlob, *Historical Thinking in South Asia: A Handbook of Sources from Colonial Times to the Present* (also published as *Sources of Historical Thinking in Modern South Asia*, 2003); Ranajit Guha, *Dominance With-out Hegemony: History and Power in Colonial India* (1997); Benjamin Elman, *From Philosophy to Philology: Intellectual and Social Aspects of Change in Late Imperial China*, 2nd rev. ed. (2001); and Margaret Mehl, *History and the State in Nineteenth-Century Japan* (1998).

POSTMODERN HISTORIOGRAPHY

Historiography has not been untouched by the difficult concepts often lumped under the names "postmodernism" or "poststructuralism." Insofar as these are not mere terms of abuse, they might most appropriately apply in Keith Jenkins, *Why History?: Ethics and Postmodernity* (1999); and to the essays collected in Keith Jenkins (ed.), *The Postmodern History Reader* (1997). Jenkins is a radical skeptic about the referentiality of language, which of course calls all historical statements into question. Those who do not go this far have nevertheless become interested in "modernist events," those which defy the powers of historiography (at least as conventionally practiced) to represent them. The Holocaust is of course the prime example, but far from the only one. The best treatments are to be found in some of the essays in Hayden White, *Figural Realism: Studies in the Mimesis Effect* (1999); and in Frank Ankersmit, *Sublime Historical Experience* (2005).